D

# CONTEMPORARY THEORIES IN THE SOCIOLOGY OF EDUCATION

# CONTEMPORARY
# THEORIES IN
# THE SOCIOLOGY OF
# EDUCATION

Jack Demai

M

*First edition 1981*
*Reprinted 1982, 1983*

*Published by*
THE MACMILLAN PRESS LTD
*London and Basingstoke*
*Companies and representatives*
*throughout the world*

*Printed in Hong Kong*

British Library Cataloguing in Publication Data

Demaine, Jack
   Contemporary theories in the sociology of
   education
   1.   Educational sociology
   I.   Title
   301.5'6        LC191

   ISBN 0–333–23448–0
   ISBN 0–333–23449–9 Pbk

TO MY PARENTS

# Contents

# List of Tables

# Figure

# Acknowledgements

I should like to thank all those who have contributed to this book through their criticism and comment. They are too numerous to mention by name but I am nonetheless grateful to them all. I would like especially to thank Lorraine Culley and Barry Hindess who both read the manuscript in full and made extremely helpful suggestions.

I am grateful to the Editors of *Economy and Society* and to the publishers, Messrs Routledge & Kegan Paul Ltd, for permission to reproduce parts of a paper first published in Volume 6, Number 2 of that journal. I am also grateful to the Controller of Her Majesty's Stationery Office for permission to reproduce the tables from the Diamond Report and the Taylor Report.

# Introduction

In recent years sociology of education has been transformed and the state of theoretical debate invigorated by the influx of Marxist, neo-Marxist and radical theories and concepts. This book distinguishes between these theories and concepts and examines their influence. The book examines the 'traditional' as well as the 'new' sociology of education and goes on to examine attempts to develop a 'Marxist sociology of education'.

The book examines and criticizes the so-called New Directions for the sociology of education proposed by Michael F. D. Young, Louis Althusser's elaboration of the concept of the educational ideological state apparatus, and Bowles and Gintis' attempt to establish a 'political economy' of education. There is an extended examination and criticism of Parsonian concepts which appear in the traditional sociology and a critique of influential aspects of the work of Emile Durkheim and Basil Bernstein. The chapter on Marxist sociology of education includes a critique of the theoretical concepts at work in Paulo Freire's discourse on education and in the following chapter there is a critique of the allegedly radical alternatives for education proposed by Ivan Illich.

The objective of the book is to demonstrate the serious theoretical limitations of these and other similar approaches and to examine the consequences for pedagogic practice entailed in the implementation of policies based on such theories. Finally, in chapter 6 there is an assessment of the current state of sociology of education and a discussion of the contemporary debate on education in Britain with specific reference to the educational politics of the Left.

## (i) MARXIST THEORY AND SOCIOLOGY OF EDUCATION

There has, in recent years, been considerable theoretical interest in the development of a Marxist sociology of education. The fact that the founders of Marxism (Marx and Engels) and the major exponent of Marxism in the twentieth century (Lenin) had little to say on the subject is not in itself a serious obstacle to such a development because there are other Marxists who have written on education, and there are Marxist concepts which might be brought to work in educational theory. The most serious attempt in recent years to advance Marxist theory beyond the works of Marx, Engels and Lenin, that of the French philosopher Louis Althusser, includes an attempt to extend Marxist theory to educational theory. On the other hand, in Britain, Maurice Levitas' *Marxist Perspectives in the Sociology of Education* attempts to combine certain of Marx and Engels' asides and comments on education (Lenin seems to have slipped his notice) with sociological concepts. Despite his explicit hostility to *some* sociology the results owe much to sociology and in particular to a speculative philosophical anthropology.

A Marxist sociology of education which utilizes Marx and Engels' asides on education faces an issue which is also prevalent in Lenin's comments and speeches on education. For these writers, satisfactory education for the working people is not possible in bourgeois capitalist society. On the other hand, education is considered to be of considerable importance in the transition to socialism. This apparent paradox has led to considerable problems for Marxist, neo-Marxist and radical theories of education. Of course, there is no paradox for classical Marxism because the transition to socialism presupposes revolution; the seizure and transformation of the bourgeois state and the transformation of capitalist economies to socialist economies. Let us examine Lenin's arguments on education by way of illustration.

In his speech[1] at the First All-Russian Congress on Education (28 August 1918) Lenin argued that 'the more cultured the bourgeois state, the more subtly it lied when declaring that schools could stand above politics and serve society as a whole. In fact the schools were turned into nothing but an instrument of the class rule of the bourgeoisie. They were thoroughly imbued with the bourgeois caste spirit.' The revolution means that 'education is one of the component parts of the struggle we are now waging'. Here education is political in the sense that it is imbued with caste spirit and schools are an instrument of the ruling class. Lenin's opposition to schooling is an opposition to its bourgeois class basis and ideology. Lenin is not opposed to education as such.

Lenin's position is not that education is to be opposed because it is necessarily political in character but rather that politics *presupposes education*. The political ideology or 'caste spirit' of the bourgeoisie does not exist in isolation from the instruments in which it is imbued. Lenin's arguments (in 1921) are consistent with this position and, with respect to the objectives of socialism, he again . argues that political thought and political action presuppose education.

In admonishing the members of the Political Education Departments for their choice of the pretentious title of 'political educationalists', Lenin argued that 'so long as there is such a thing as illiteracy in our country it is too much to talk about political education. This is not a political problem; it is a condition without which it is useless talking about politics. An illiterate person stands outside politics, he must first learn his ABC.'[2]

Lenin does not mean that literacy qualifications be set up to disenfranchise the illiterate. Nor does he mean that the question of the struggle for the conditions necessary for the education of the people is not a political question. Rather, Lenin means that those who do not have such basic skills as literacy place themselves outside politics, or better, they are placed outside politics by the policies which lead to conditions in which they are deprived of basic education. Such are the policies implied in the political education-alists' notion that their task is primarily one of political education, which is precisely why Lenin admonished them.

Now, it is clear that the tasks which faced educationalists in the Soviet Union in 1921 cannot be equated with those with which educationalists in Britain are faced in the late 70s and the 1980s. For example, it is not at all the case that in Britain today political education would not be an appropriate subject on the curriculum. The differences between Britain in the late 70s and in the 80s and the Soviet Union in 1921 are rather too numerous to set out in this short book, and only dogmatists would suggest that Lenin's writings could be brought *en bloc* to the analysis of modern Britain. Nevertheless, Lenin's approach to the specific issues to which he addressed himself can be instructive both for Marxists and non-Marxists in a number of respects.

Schematically, Lenin demonstrates that his party has definite objectives and specific strategies based on determinate analysis of the specific conjunc-ture. With regard to culture, education, politics and the peasants and industrial proletariat, Lenin is clear that the objective of political education presupposes and demands certain conditions of development. The objective of political education cannot be achieved overnight and the securing of certain prior conditions is therefore the initial objective. Lenin insisted that 'political education calls for raising the level of culture at all costs. The ability to read and write must be made to serve the purpose of raising the cultural level; the peasants must be able to use the ability to read and write for the improvement of their farms and their state.'[3] Lenin's remarks form part of a wider policy, and with respect to the economy his party was concerned with the effective implementation of the New Economic Policy. Of course, although Lenin regarded education as a necessary condition for the political objective of the transition to socialism, the securing of the conditions of existence of any political formation or relations of production was never reduced to the effects of the sphere of ideology or schooling, as it is in the work of some contemporary writers.

Now, although contemporary 'friends of the people', such as some of the radical sociologists, could learn much from Lenin's remarks on literacy (cf. Keddie's writing for example),[4] the main point here is that Lenin's policy on educational matters is directed at specific issues and it has definite objectives. One of the main aims of this present book is to investigate the work of contemporary sociologists, Marxists, radicals and socialists working within education to determine *their* objectives, and to show that in certain instances the consequences of the implementation of the ideas presented in their theoretical discourse are quite different from their stated objectives.

To remain with the question of Marxism, it is argued in this book that there can be no *general* Marxist theory of education. In chapter 3 Marx's own comments on education are examined. His comments on the Lassallean demands in his *Critique of the Gotha Programme* include comment on the demand for 'Universal and *equal elementary education* by the state. Universal compulsory school attendance. Free instruction' (emphasis in the original). Marx's forty lines or so of comment on the Lassallean demands, incisive and appropriate as it was to the effective criticism of the German Workers' Programme in 1875, can hardly form the basis of a general Marxist theory of education, or indeed form the basis of any strategy for contemporary educational policy formulation. Likewise with Lenin's speeches and papers recently published in a collection under the title *On Public Education*. Indeed, rather than providing the basis for any general theory or strategy Lenin's speeches and papers and Marx's writings on education are exemplary in their demonstration that strategies and policies must be appropriate to determinate conjunctures.

It might be suggested that despite the objections raised above (and specifically the argument that Marx and Engels had little to say about education), a general Marxist theory of education *is* possible. After all, there are numerous Marxists who have written on education and there are certain Marxist concepts which might be used to construct such a general theory. There are two major problems here. On the one hand there is the question of 'general theory' as such, and on the other there is the question of the theoretical status of those general concepts which are supposed to make up that general theory.

A project for a general theory proposes a finite field of general concepts from which further concepts and deductions are made. Those general concepts are conceived of as having theoretical primacy in discourse and are therefore conceived of as serving as absolute criteria governing the formation of less general concepts. Thus the proposal for a 'general theory' as such represents a rationalist and ultimately dogmatic conception of the nature of the objects of discourse. [5] In its most extreme forms the project for a general theory implies the establishment of theoretical discourse without reference to decisions, events, calculations and the carrying out of effective policies etc. in that sphere in which such a general theory is proposed. Issues in current educational policy cannot be ignored. The suppression of the consideration of such decisions, usually with reference to them as insignificant effects of 'social-democratic reformism' illustrates the obstacles inherent in certain conceptions of general Marxist theory of education. The argument against the dogmatism and rationalism of general theory here does not imply an 'anti-theoretical' position in the sense that the only alternative is an equally dogmatic 'empiricist' conception of the objects of discourse. Neither general theoretical concepts nor 'empirical events' can be dispensed with. Each represents a level of conceptualization in discourse, but neither represents a privileged level or source of deductions. The potentially disastrous consequences of dogmatism for policy formation within the sphere of discourse on education is a recurring theme in this book.

Now, on the question of a general Marxist theory of education and the objections to such a theory it is clear that there can be no *a priori* objection to Marxist theory in general in the sense of a body of theoretical concepts and relations between such concepts. However, concepts which are central to and sometimes referred to as the 'basic concepts' of Marxism such as the concepts of mode of production, relations of production, social formation etc. and relations between them, have been subject to severe theoretical scrutiny in recent years. This theoretical scrutiny has revealed discrepancies and ambiguities within certain of these concepts and in the relations between them. Since a precise unitary theoretical status cannot be derived from the ambiguous and theoretically incoherent concepts in classical Marxism, it must follow that no general Marxist theory of education can be derived from the 'basic concepts' of Marxism.

Now, many of the general concepts which certain writers attempt to bring to the construction of a general theory are themselves not without problems. It will be shown that the work of such writers as Althusser and followers such as Paulo Freire brings with it many of the theoretical problems from Marxism which are no less of a problem when 'applied' to the analysis of education. The sociologists of education who have enthusiastically embraced 'Althusserianism' have, unwittingly in many instances, embraced more problems than solutions. Despite the considerable sophistication and theoretical rigour of Althusser's work in comparison to most of the sociology of education, the solutions which sociologists seek in Althusser's work and in the work of other Marxists, and indeed in Marx

himself, frequently involve the adoption of internally theoretically in-
adequate Marxist concepts and theories: typically, the concept of alienation
and Marx's philosophical anthropology, the theory of ideology[6] and the
related problems in Althusser's concept of 'structural causality'. We will
return to some of these theoretical problems in chapter 3. For the moment let
us now consider the work of M. F. D. Young and his proposals for radical
New Directions for the sociology of education.

## (ii)  RADICALISM AND THE NEW SOCIOLOGY OF EDUCATION

The publication of the book *Knowledge and Control* edited by Young and
containing a number of contributions by the editor, heralded in its subtitle
the 'new directions for the sociology of education'. The new directions
suggested in that publication were similar to those suggested elsewhere. The
new directions for sociological theory set out in the book edited by Filmer et
al. and titled *New Directions in Sociological Theory*, for example, were said to
involve a 'radical reorientation of sociology'. A primary feature of this
reorganization is the adoption of a phenomenological perspective.

     One of the main concerns of the new sociology of education, and
particularly the concern of the writings of Young, is with the alleged *political*
character of educational knowledge. In the paper titled *On the Politics of
Educational Knowledge*, Young contends that educational knowledge is to be
conceived of as a construct of 'underlying meanings' and, as such, a reflection
of certain political interests. The task of the New Directions is the
exploration of the social construction of meanings and it is Young's claim
that this task can be accomplished by following the 'phenomenological'
and philosophical works of Alfred Schutz. Part of the aim of this present
book is to challenge Young's project by examining his contention that
knowledge is 'socially constructed' and examining the precise character of
the alleged 'radicalism' of the new sociology of education. It is argued in this
book that the radical attack on the political character of contemporary
education cannot be sustained and it is demonstrated that the categories
which Young uses to designate himself and the character of his work, that is,
as radical and socialist, are, within his discourse, quite vacuous. It is not
argued that Young is not a socialist or that his work is not radical in
character, but rather that within his own discourse these notions are
indeterminate.

     Young's work takes the form of 'guidelines' for the new directions for the
sociology of education, and the reader is referred to the work of numerous
authors whose work might be adopted in order to develop this new
sociology of education. A major difficulty with Young's writings is the

schematic nature of these guides and the cryptic character of the references he makes to other writers. Such references are often a substitute for argument, and the problem becomes quite serious when it is found that the concepts to which we are referred fail to support the point to which they are brought, or are themselves theoretically incoherent. This book follows up some of Young's references and guides for the development of the sociology of the politics of educational knowledge, and finds that they are not the direction for any advance in the sociology of education.

In *Knowledge and Control* Young argues that sociological research drawing on the Marxist, Weberian and Durkheimian tradition can contribute to a reorientation of the sociology of education. Since the new sociology takes its methodology from the 'phenomenological' sociology of Alfred Schutz, and the latter is little more than a one-sided development of Weber's methodological views, we can agree that the new sociology of education is at least in part, rooted in the Weberian tradition. [7] A major theoretical problem arises in precisely how it is possible to *combine* the discourse of Marx, Weber and Durkheim, or even elements drawn from their mutually exclusive theoretical discourse. In addition to this problem, to which Young offers no solution, there is the not inconsiderable problem that, as we have already commented, Marx for example offers no systematic elaboration of a theory of education. Young points to the work of Paulo Freire to provide the Marxist ingredient for the concoction which is to reorient the sociology of education. This book examines the theoretical structure of Freire's discourse, with particular reference to his theory of education and to his concept of politics. Young claims to subscribe to Freire's concept of politics and this indication is important because although the former is explicitly concerned with the concept of politics, his own writings render his conception of politics indeterminable. However, Young says that he uses the term 'political' in Paulo Freire's sense that all action is political.

Young's use of Freire to illustrate his own concept of politics raises considerable theoretical problems which are not exclusive to that use or to Freire's own discourse, although they are highlighted in the latter. They have their origin in some of Marx's own conceptualizations of the reproduction of social formations and of their transformation, and they have been repeated in the work of some later Marxists. These problems involve the postulation of contradictory formulations of a teleological conception of the reproduction of the social formation (exemplified in Althusser's concept of 'structural causality'), and a teleological conception of the necessary transformation of the social formation, and the consequent denegation of politics and political struggle. These theoretical problems are discussed further in the book; for the moment they can only be noted schematically. A schematic though clear example of the teleology of some of Marx's own conceptualization of the transition from one mode of production to another, which constitutes part of this theoretical problem, can be found in Marx's 1859 Preface to *A Contribution to the Critique of Political Economy*.[8] Here 'social revolution', for example the transition from the dominance of the capitalist mode of production in a social formation and the transition to socialism, is conceived in a teleological fashion in which politics and political struggle play no effective part. Indeed, here 'political and intellectual life' are conditioned by 'the mode of production of material life' and the 'entire immense superstructure' which in Marx's formulation here includes politics and political thought, is transformed as an effect of the 'change of the economic foundation'. It is against precisely such formulations as these that Lenin argued so vehemently in his critique of 'economism' and his insistence on politics and on political struggle.[9]

Although Freire is explicitly concerned with politics, as we shall see in chapter 3, he restricts politics to the cultural actions of radicals who, in his own formulations, are not strictly necessary to his conception of transition (i.e. transition from capitalism to socialism), although the latter is nevertheless conceived in terms of their actions. The cultural actions of radicals are conceived as *both* necessary and unnecessary. Freire's discourse conflates and combines a teleological conception of the 'humanization of man' with the teleological conception of the transition of social formations 'borrowed' from some forms of Marxism. This is posited together with a teleological conception of 'structural causality' which is borrowed from Marxism via the work of Louis Althusser.[10] Thus, a teleological conception of reproduction of the social formation is posited together with a teleological conception of transition. Freire's discourse serves as a clear example of the use of such teleological concepts and as an example of the theoretical problems which must arise as a consequence of the theorization of contradictory conceptions within the same discourse.

The main conclusion of the radical critique of the politics of educational knowledge is that, in Young's terms, education is the 'imposition of meanings' whilst in Freire's terms it is an 'instrument of oppression'. The elaboration of such notions poses similar theoretical problems to those raised by Althusser's elaboration of the function of the educational ideological state apparatus.[11] In addition to those problems the radical critique raises the issue of precisely what form of analysis of contemporary education, and what type of educational policy is consequent on its formulations of the function of education. Young is concerned that the radical critique should lead to the development of educational alternatives, and he refers his readers to Illich's *Deschooling Society*. The question of the 'radicalism' of Illich's suggestions and the 'deschooling' position is discussed in chapter 4. For the moment it should be noted that this position is not a Marxist position drawn between Marxism and the radical critique of contemporary educational systems. Marxism is concerned with the analysis of determinate conjunctures as well as theory of social formations, and it is clear that the formulation education = ideology is not an adequate Marxist analysis of the function of education in contemporary capitalist society. Such a formulation leads to, or at least leaves the way open to, an opposition to educational systems and to support for so-called 'radical alternatives' such as the deschooling programme presented in the work of Illich. Contrary to the formulation education = ideology and the notion that education is necessarily political in character, as in Young's sense that it is essentially the imposition of class meanings and the interests of the ruling class, many Marxists (and notably Lenin as we have seen) as well as non-Marxists, argue that politics presuppose education.

In conclusion it should be noted that on the issue of political education as a subject on the curriculum Young is silent. For him all education is necessarily political irrespective of its content. The critique of Young's formulations in chapter 2 consists of a critique of his *sociology* of the politics of educational knowledge. It is no part of my critique to argue against political education and neither do I argue that education is not political in the sense of having no political effects. In the concluding chapter I insist that educational policy and pedagogic practice are subject to political debate and to political struggle and suggest means of conceptualizing arenas of such debate and struggle.

## (iii) EDUCATION AND EDUCATIONAL POLICY: THEORY AND MODES OF CRITIQUE OF THEORETICAL DISCOURSE

Educational policy, or indeed any policy, presupposes theory. This book has two objectives; on the one hand to investigate theories themselves, and on the other to investigate the consequences for educational provision and for pedagogic practice of policies based on such theories. In examining theories themselves the investigation is concerned strictly with the internal structure of the concepts and theories involved. That is to say, it is directed at the internal, logical and conceptual problems and inadequacies of the concepts and theories concerned. [12]

Educational theories (not only in sociology of course) provide the means of analysis of education and they also provide the means of conceptualizing and setting out objectives for reforms and changes in educational policy. Since policy presupposes theory it is appropriate that the coherence of theories and concepts be examined and the implications for policy assessed.

Incoherent theories have little to offer in the analysis of issues and problems, and can provide little in the way of serious solutions and policy. The theories examined and criticized in this book are concerned with significant issues but they often fail to pose these issues in a fruitful way.

This book is concerned, then, with theories at two levels. On the one hand it is concerned with theories themselves and with a mode of critique which is strictly internal and theoretical. On the other hand it is concerned with the consequences for educational provision and pedagogic practice entailed in the implementation of policies based on such theories. This latter form of criticism necessarily involves conceptions of what the important issues and problems are in contemporary education. It involves assessment of how successful certain theories are in terms of making significant contributions to the posing of questions and problems, and in providing the basis for serious solutions. For example, it is argued that the formulations of some radical sociologists of education lead to an antagonism towards contemporary education. As we shall see in chapter 2 the arguments presented by Nell Keddie in her discussion of 'the concept of cultural deprivation' lead to a pedagogy which involves the deprivation of children of their formal education.

It may well be that it was not the 'intention' of these authors to argue for that which is the logical consequence of their discourse and they may explicitly reject the consequences implied in that theoretical discourse. In this book the wills and intentions of authors are not of primary interest. Indeed, it is not the authors that are under investigation but theories and the consequences of theories for educational practice. In as much as authors are mentioned by name it is merely in order to identify their discourse.

Many of the authors whose discourse is criticized make claims that their work is Marxist, or radical, or that they are socialists working within education. Young uses the last two categories to describe his work, whilst Bowles and Gintis on the other hand claim, in their book *Schooling in Capitalist America*, that they are 'impressed' by certain of 'Marx's observations' and suggest that their work is influenced by Marxism. Their book is strewn with references to and quotations from the works of Marx. In his book *Deschooling Society* Illich maintains that he is a radical who 'hopes for fundamental change' and he argues that 'a political programme which does not explicitly recognise the need for deschooling is not revolutionary'. In their most recent publication *Society, State and Schooling*, Young and Whitty conclude that they 'hope that a more adequate analysis of the relations between society, state and schooling will emerge . . . and that socialists working within education and elsewhere will begin to develop more realistic strategies for change'.

In criticizing these and other authors we are concerned with their theoretical discourse and its consequences for education rather than with their 'hopes', 'wills' or 'intentions'. The hope of many of these authors is for 'socialism', for 'revolution' or for some form of radical change. They are concerned with the struggle for certain of these objectives in the sphere of education, and one of their major concerns is with working class education and with the 'interests' of the working class in general. It is argued in this book that in some cases these concerns are articulated in forms which amount to little more than rhetoric and empty slogans. In some cases, however, the arguments could lead to policies which would deprive working class children and youth of their formal education. This is particularly the case in some of the arguments found in the work of Young, Keddie and Illich for example.

The discussion of the consequences of certain theoretical formulations for pedagogic practice is, however, only part of the critical discussion which appears in the following chapters, albeit an important and indeed crucial discussion. A major part of the argument which appears in this book is concerned with theories; with their internal structure and with their internal, logical and conceptual problems and inadequacies. With respect to this mode of critique and to the criticism of certain authors who represent themselves as Marxist, radicals or socialists, a number of comments are necessary in order to avoid misunderstanding. Let us take the question of Marxist authors from the above, by way of an example.

The form of criticism adopted does not attempt to measure the discourses under investigation against some privileged theoretical discourse or 'meta-discourse'. Such a strategy would leave open the question of the precise theoretical status of the privileged discourse on the one hand or the 'validity' of the 'meta-discourse' on the other. This then leaves open the question of the mode of 'validation' or the determination of the status of discourses which were deemed privileged, and so on in an infinite regression. In the criticism of Marxists and their discourse it is not, therefore, the claim of the present writer that such discourses are 'invalid' because they diverge from classical Marxist theory. Much of what appears under the heading of Marxism is, however, clearly so far removed as to have nothing whatever to do with Marxism, save for the use of words and some slogans which resemble those in Marxist discourse. Nevertheless, such an observation cannot and does not constitute a critique. It is argued here that *no* theoretical discourse can bestow upon itself, or have bestowed on it by others, the status of privilege which suggests that such a discourse represents the 'real' or the 'true facts'. No discourse, whether Marxist or non-Marxist can be dismissed merely because of its divergence from classical Marxism. Indeed, no theoretical discourse can be criticized through a comparison with another theory or supposed privileged level of discourse without avoiding the problem of dogmatism.

In this book then, theories are not criticized by comparing them with other theories or other levels of discourse. Such a mode of critique, an epistemological mode, is always dogmatic because it supposes a privileged level of discourse against which the theories to be criticized are compared and examined. Positivist epistemology supposes a privileged level of discourse which is said to represent the 'real' 'empirical facts'. Determinate discourses are alleged to be 'false' or 'wrong' or 'unreal' if they fail to comply with what is alleged to be the 'real' 'empirical facts'. The problem is that what appear as the empirical facts of the real world are themselves the product of determinate discursive accounts which themselves presuppose theories. This is not to argue that there is no real empirical world outside of discourse, nor that there is no possibility of valuable and significant empirical evidence, but simply that there can be no account of the phenomena of the world outside discourse. The latter always involves theories and theoretical concepts.

In non-positivist epistemology it is alleged that certain theories are 'false' or 'incorrect' because they fail to recognize objects specified in other theoretical discourse. For example, some Marxists base their critique of the theories of social scientists or 'bourgeois' historians on their failure to recognize the objects specified in Marxist discourse. Rather than constituting a critique, this mode of analysis simply measures the distance between the objects specified in one discourse and those specified in another. Epistemology *always* poses some level of discourse of a privileged status. The precise determination of such alleged privilege may vary from account to account, for example, may be said to derive from an 'extra-discursive' or 'meta-theoretical' level, from 'science', from 'Historical Materialism', from 'givens' (Durkheim) or, as in positivist epistemology, from the 'empirical' 'facts' of the 'real' world.

Criticism of the theories and arguments that appear in the pages of this book then, is directed at the internal, logical and conceptual problems and inadequacies of the theory concerned. Theories are not criticized by comparing them with other theories which are supposed to represent privileged levels of theory or to the 'real' world. The mode of critique is not therefore a 'realist' or an 'empiricist' mode which alleges to measure theories against the 'real', 'empirical' 'facts' or against some conception of the 'real' posited by some meta-theory.

(iv) STRUCTURE OF THE BOOK

The structure of the book is as follows. The first chapter is concerned with some of the main concepts in the traditional sociology of education. It critically discusses the concepts of social institution, culture and socialization in the work of Durkheim and Parsons. It also examines the traditional sociological accounts of class, culture and language in education with specific reference to Bernstein's work. Chapter 2 examines Michael F. D. Young's project for the sociological investigation of what he argues is a major focus of political power in society; the organization of educational knowledge. It will be argued that his project, based on the 'phenomenological' sociology of Alfred Schutz, does not provide the means for assessing the political character of education. The chapter goes on to investigate the specific character of what Young refers to as 'radicalism'. The *word* radical, of course, lends itself to numerous and varied postures in both political and non-political spheres. Young uses the notion of radicalism to designate an epistemology as well as in reference to politics. Young's epistemological arguments are discussed and there is an examination of the arguments of the radical sociologist of education, Nell Keddie, on the notion of 'cultural deprivation'.

Chapter 3 examines the role of Marxist concepts in the sociology of education with specific reference to Althusser's theory of ideology and Freire's conception of the pedagogy of the oppressed. Chapter 4 discusses Illich's conception of the role of education in his concept of social change, and chapter 5 examines Bowles and Gintis' critique of Illich and their attempt to elaborate relations between the economy and the educational system in capitalist societies. The sixth and concluding chapter is concerned with educational policy and the politics of the Left in Britain and the significance of educational policy in the struggle for socialism.

# 1 Concepts in Sociology of Education

Modern sociology of education borrows and utilizes concepts from sociological theory, philosophy, economics, political theory, social anthropology, psychoanalysis and psychology. The object of this chapter is to examine and assess some of the main theoretical concepts at work in what has become known as the 'traditional' sociology of education.

It is often argued that the traditional conceptual framework in sociology of education owes much to the French sociologist Emile Durkheim. It is also clear that the work of the American sociologist Talcott Parsons has figured significantly in the traditional theoretical framework. Section A of this chapter consists of a brief discussion of Durkheim's work in sociological theory and its relation to his sociology of education. In section B there is a more detailed examination of some of the concepts elaborated in Parsonian sociology which have particular significance for the sociology of education. Parsons' work represents one of the most serious attempts to establish general theory in sociology and yet despite its high level of theoretical sophistication it is often either summarily dismissed or simply ignored by contemporary sociologists. Nevertheless, Parsons' work has had some influence in sociology of education and in this chapter it is given a detailed examination and its limitations are discussed. Finally, in section C there is an examination of British sociology of education with particular reference to its uses of the concepts of class, culture and language.

Sociology of education is concerned with the family, the education system, the economy and the polity, and with relations between them. It is concerned with social institutions and with the socialization process with which they are involved. There is a specific concern with the interrelated issues of the socialization of human individuals and the selection and allocation of individuals within the role-structure of adult society; what Parsons calls a 'dual problem'. British sociology of education is concerned with the social class differentials in the conditions of socialization and educational opportunity, and with the social class differentials in educational achievement. Schematically, the process of socialization is conceived of as involving the family and the educational system as major social institutions which transmit culture from one generation to another. Social institutions are variously conceived of as consisting of material and cultural (in the case of Durkheim, spiritual) spheres or realms. The educational system as a social institution consists of a sphere of material objects or things such as bricks and mortar, desks, blackboards, books, the salaries of teachers, lecturers, caretakers, administrators etc. and also of a cultural sphere. The term culture is used in a technical sense to refer to shared norms, values, meanings etc. and language is conceived of as an important aspect of culture. In some accounts language is classified as a social institution[1] and in others as an aspect of culture transmitted by social institutions. However classified, language, culture, the family, the education system and the economy and their interrelations are the primary concern of sociology of education.

The concept of culture appears in sociology of education as a concept within theories of socialization. The socialization process is conceived of as the process of the construction of the consciousness of the human subject through its internalization of culture. Theories of socialization purport to be theories of the subject. Although the precise character of concepts and relations between concepts vary in different theories of socialization, all such theories meet with a problem of the theoretical designation of the concept of the human subject in the process. That is, the concept of the process of socialization presupposes that the concept of the subject is designated certain attributes. It invests the concept of the subject with the capacity for cognition necessary for recognition, without which the socialization process cannot work. The problem is immediately clear; the sociological theory of socialization purports to be the theory of the construction of the consciousness and capacities of consciousness of human subjects, yet in order for such a theory to work it must of necessity presuppose such capacities in the human subject.

Those sociologists of education who see this as a problem resort to one of a number of 'solutions' at various levels of theoretical sophistication. At one level there is a resort to some version of George Herbert Mead's[2] 'role theory' and 'symbolic interactionism' and at another, to the 'structural-functionalism' of Talcott Parsons and Robert K. Merton. More recently, 'solutions' have been sought in the works of the French philosopher Louis Althusser. We shall return in detail to Althusser in chapter 3. For the moment it is sufficient to note that much of the concern with theories of socialization forms part of a more general theoretical concern with the issue of 'social control' or some variant of the so-called Hobbesian 'problem of order'. Whilst Parsons seeks theoretical solutions to the problems of socialization theory in Freud's psychoanalysis and in the combining of psychoanalytic theory with social systems theory, Althusser, in his theory of ideology, resorts to Jacques Lacan's concept of the 'mirror phase'.[3]

British sociology of education has concerned itself largely with a level at which the culture/socialization/internalization process 'works'. It has been concerned with the social class differentials in the material and cultural conditions of socialization. The social class differentials in educational achievement are attributed to differences in the conditions of socialization; to school and family and specifically to relations between them. A major concern has been with the underachievement of children from the working class in relation to the educational achievement of middle class children.[4]

Let us begin with a discussion of some of the main theoretical concepts in the work of Durkheim and Parsons and then proceed to an examination of the concerns of the traditional sociology of education in Britain. This will give us an outline of the sociology of education in which recent theories have intervened.

## A. THE CONCEPT OF SOCIAL INSTITUTION IN DURKHEIM'S SOCIOLOGY

Durkheim is regarded as one of the 'founding fathers' of sociology and his sociological theory is abstract and philosophical. It may seem inappropriate to some readers for his theoretical work to be discussed, however briefly, in a book which purports to be concerned with *contemporary* theories of education. However, Banks in *The Sociology of Education* contends that 'the traditional conceptual framework in the subject is that of functionalism, and derives primarily from the writings of the French sociologist Emile Durkheim'. Since Durkheim is considered to be one of the founding fathers of sociology and of the sociology of education, and since he was concerned specifically with sociology as 'the science of institutions', a brief consideration of his theoretical work is indeed appropriate.[5]

In the Preface to the Second Edition of his book *The Rules of Sociological Method*, Durkheim defines his concept of institution and of society. He designates 'as "institutions" all the beliefs and all the modes of conduct instituted by the collectivity' and contends that 'sociology can then be defined as the science of institutions, of their genesis and their functioning' (p. lvi). In the *Rules* Durkheim attempts to legislate for the conditions of production of 'scientific' sociological knowledge. For Durkheim the latter is based on the 'fundamental principle' that 'social facts' are 'things' of 'objective reality'. These facts should be studied as they present themselves, as *things*, in a strictly objective manner.

For Durkheim the facts of the social are a united and equivalent 'field' as a result of their being alike phenomena or manifestations of deeper causes. Durkheim's field of 'given facts' presuppose an essence, in the absence of which they become a more or less random collection of facts. It is possible to know the essence through the study of the phenomena because of the necessary connection between the phenomena and their essence (the given facts and their cause). Durkheim *already knows the nature of the essence* that underlies the phenomena. Social facts are phenomena of the 'collective conscience' and its states.

In Durkheim's concept of social structure the collective conscience or the collective sentiments are conceived of as a living essence which is manifested in particular phenomena. 'Institutions' are merely 'crystallised' expressions of the collective sentiments, given this form through habit and repetition. The social 'whole' for Durkheim is thus an essentially spiritual whole, the unity of the collective conscience, and its 'parts' or 'phenomena' are manifestations of the nature of the whole. They reflect the action of the collective sentiments. Thus it is possible to 'know' the essence from the phenomena for they are the mere scene of its action.[6]

Now although Durkheim's contribution to sociology of education may seem at first glance to consist merely of 'practical prescriptions' it is nevertheless permeated with the theoretical problems which are a consequence of the essentialism of his general sociology. In *Education and Sociology* Durkheim considers that the term 'education' should be reserved for,

> the influence exercised by adult generations on those that are not yet ready for social life. Its object is to arouse and to develop in the child a certain number of physical, intellectual and moral states which are demanded of him by both the political society as a whole and the special milieu for which he is specifically destined. (p. 71; emphasis in original)

Durkheim is concerned with the process of this educational influence, its source and its function. They are found immediately. He insists that,

> we cannot and we must not all be devoted to the same kind of life, we have, according to our aptitudes, different functions to fulfil, and we must adapt ourselves to what we must do [and] it is not we as individuals who have created the customs and ideas that determine this type [of education]. They are the product of a common life, and they express its needs. (p. 62)

Happy contingency fits the presupposed aptitudes of human individuals and the needs expressed by society (common life). The individual's aptitudes always already express the needs of society, his 'destiny'. The 'needs' of society are secured as an effect of functional customs and sets of ideas expressed in the educational 'influence of adults on youth', who are always already inclined towards the needs of society. Given this predisposition, a consequence of Durkheim's conceptualization, material mechanisms would seem superfluous. He offers empirical identification of them all the same.

Durkheim argues that the socialization process involved in education is vital. It is 'the means by which society prepares, within the children, the *essential conditions of its very existence*' (p. 71). These conditions of existence of society involve securing both diversity and uniformity, and are facilitated by the existence of a 'dual being' in each individual human subject, the constitution of the totality of which is the end of education.

> society can survive only if there exists among its members a sufficient degree of homogeneity; education perpetuates and reinforces this homogeneity by fixing in the child, from the beginning, the essential similarities that collective life demands. But on the other hand, without a certain diversity all co-operation would be impossible; education assures the persistence of this necessary diversity by being itself diversified and specialised. (p. 70)

Diversity is both necessary and the mere manifestation of a deeper essential uniformity. Diversity and uniformity are merely degrees of manifestation of an essential nature, the collective conscience. The diversity of the complex social whole is bound together by the moral unity of the collective conscience. The collective conscience or collective sentiments are conceived as a living essence which manifests itself in institutions which are, as we have seen, merely crystallized expressions of the collective sentiments formed by ritual and practice.

In Durkheim's conception of the social whole as an essentially moral or spiritual unity this unity secures, in its expression in social phenomena, the conditions of existence of the social whole—its own unity. Durkheim's use of metaphors and analogies with the biological sciences in his sociology performs a metonymic function of inference of a material to an essentially spiritual unity. It imputes to the expressive causality of his classical philosophy of 'society' a mode of structural causality. As we shall see in a later chapter, Louis Althusser's attempt to break with the expressive causality of classical philosophy by a mere rewriting is not dissimilar to Durkheim's use of an overlying metaphorical system. Whilst Althusser merely writes in 'structural causality' for expressive causality, Durkheim 'hides' his expressive causality behind the biological analogy and metaphor. No such masks can hide the teleological character of these conceptions. The teleological character of Durkheim's conception of the *guaranteed* securing of the conditions of existence of the unity of the social whole by its own unity, or additionally by social institutions and by the 'material' means of education has been demonstrated above. We shall return to Althusser in chapter 3.


## B. TALCOTT PARSONS AND THE SOCIOLOGY OF EDUCATION

The significance of the work of Talcott Parsons for sociology of education centres on concepts which appear in his conceptualization of the school class as a social system in the paper titled 'The School Class as a Social System: Some of Its Functions in American Society'.[7] The important concepts of socialization, internalization, allocation and differentiation, and the concepts of personality, social and cultural systems utilized in that paper are more elaborately specified elsewhere in, for example, *Towards a General Theory of Action* and in what Parsons refers to as its 'second volume', *The Social System*.[8]

In conceptualizing the school class as a social system, Parsons utilizes the abstract concept of social system which, together with the personality and cultural system, form the three systems of action which are unified in his theoretical work by the action 'frame of reference'. The frame of reference of the theory of action involves actors, a situation of action and the orientation of action. The theory of action is said to be a conceptual scheme for the analysis of the behaviour of living organisms. The theory of action conceives of the behaviour of living organisms as oriented to the attainment of 'ends' or 'goals' in situations by means of the normatively regulated expenditure of energy or motivation. The action frame of reference is concerned with the orientation of actors (human individuals—in the fundamental case biological organisms) to a situation which includes other actors. In the case of the school class as a social system these other actors will be the teacher and pupils. Action is the action of an actor and it takes place in a situation consisting of objects. These objects may be other actors or physical or cultural objects. The system of relations-to-objects which each actor has is called his 'system of orientations' and the objects may be goal objects, resources, means, conditions, obstacles or symbols. Objects, by the cathexes[9] and significances attached to them, become *organized* into the actor's system of orientations. Parsons is concerned with the organization of action into a system.

Despite the analytic separation of action into elements, actions are not empirically discrete but occur in constellations which are called systems.

Parsons is concerned with three systems; that is, with three modes of organization of the elements of action. These elements of action are organized as social systems or organizations of 'role-expectations', personalities or organizations of 'need-dispositions' and as cultural systems or organizations of 'value-orientations'. Personalities and social systems are conceived as modes of organization of 'motivated' action; personalities are systems of motivated action organized around living organisms, whilst social systems are systems of motivated action organized around the relations of actors to each other. However, cultural systems are conceived as systems of symbolic patterns. The elements of this system are internalized within the personality system and institutionalized within the social system. Parsons argues that whilst the three systems are analytically separate they are not empirically discrete or 'concretely' separable and all three are involved in the same concrete action.

The school class as a social system is a system of action and involves a process of *inter*action between actors, between teacher and pupils and between pupil and pupils. Parsons is explicitly opposed to any conflation of distinct analytical levels, that is, to the treatment of social systems as only the 'resultants' of personalities as in the writings of those of a 'psychological' viewpoint because it ignores the *organization* of action about the exigencies of a social system as a *system*, and on the other hand he is opposed to the treatment of social systems as only 'embodiments' of patterns of culture as is common in the writings of some anthropologists. Parsons' opposition to reduction of the social to the psychological is extended to a further opposition, for example to Durkheim's 'sociologistic' reduction of personality in the paper 'The Superego and the Theory of Social Systems',[10] and he also opposes theories which conceive of the social or psychological as merely 'emanations' from a given set of cultural patterns, for example, in the paper 'The Role of Ideas in Social Action'.[11] It is in the light of this explicit anti-reductionism that Parsons' conception of socialization and of 'internalization' will be examined.

The notion of internalization is of major significance to the conception of the school class as a social system because, together with the notion of the allocation of human resources within the role-structure of adult society, it forms what Parsons calls a 'dual problem'. Parsons represents the social division of labour as a socio-technical division and the school class as an agency of socialization.

Our main problem, then, is in a dual problem: first of how the school class functions to internalize in its pupils both the commitments and capacities for successful performance of their future adult roles, and second of how it functions to allocate these human resources within the role-structure of the adult society. (Parsons, 1964, p. 130)

The ways in which these two problems are interrelated are the main points of reference for Parsons' elaboration of the functions of the school class as a social system.

From the 'functional point of view' the school class is treated as an agency of socialization. It is an agency through which individual human personalities are trained to be motivationally and technically adequate to perform adult roles. Socialization is the development in individuals of the commitments and capacities which are essential prerequisites of their future role-performance. There are two components to commitment: commitment to the implementation of the broad values of society, and commitment to the performance of a specific type of role within the structure of society. Capacities too have two components: firstly that of competence or skill to perform the tasks involved in the individual's roles, and secondly 'role responsibility' or capacity to live up to other people's expectations of appropriate interpersonal behaviour.

Thus a mechanic as well as a doctor needs to have not only the basic 'skills of his trade', but also the ability to behave responsibly toward those people with whom he is brought into contact in his work. (ibid., p. 130)

We shall examine two aspects of the dual problem in more detail. These aspects are firstly, that of the *mechanisms* of 'internalization' of commitments and capacities, and secondly the *mechanisms* of differentiation which facilitate the allocation of 'manpower', that is, the allocation of individuals to occupational roles in adult society. The two are elements of a dual problem because selection and allocation to adult roles are accompanied by the internalization of concomitant value orientations. Part of the problem of the conceptualization of the mechanisms of internalization and the mechanisms of differentiation and allocation is the determination of the mechanisms by which value orientations are concomitant with differential occupational roles. Let us begin with the question of internalization.

(i) INTERNALIZATION

Though the school class is not the only agency, it can be regarded as a *focal* socializing agency and socialization can be regarded as the development in individuals of the commitments and capacities which are essential prerequisites of their future role-performance. Socialization, then, is the process of internalization or development in individuals of commitments and capacities. As we have just seen, both commitments and capacities have two components. We are concerned, here, with the *process* of internalization, that is, with the *mechanisms* within the socialization process.

In the paper 'The Superego and the Theory of Social Systems', in his book *Social Structure and Personality*, Parsons argues that an advance can be made in this problem by the theoretical unification of the theory of action in sociology with psychoanalysis. The starting point, for Parsons, is what he sees as the convergence of Freud's theory of the superego with Durkheim's theory of the social role of moral norms. Despite the problem that for Durkheim 'society exists only in the minds of individuals' and the problem that 'in Durkheim's work there are only suggestions relative to the psychological mechanisms of internalization and the place of internalized moral values in the structure of the personality itself', there is, nevertheless, convergence of the 'fundamental insights' of Freud and Durkheim as to the internalization of values. The formulations of Freud and Durkheim are not unproblematic and Parsons sets about certain modifications by which to encourage theoretical convergence. For one, Durkheim's formulation that 'society exists only in the minds of individuals' is an unfortunate result of 'certain terminological peculiarities' by which Durkheim, according to Parsons, 'tended to identify "society" as such with the system of moral norms'. As we have already seen, however, the theoretical problems in Durkheim's work cannot be reduced to merely 'terminological' problems.

For Parsons, the starting point for the theoretical unification he intends to promote and develop is the analysis of certain features of the interaction of persons; the process of interaction itself being conceived as a system.

> Once the essentials of such an interactive system have been made clear, the implications of the analysis can be followed out in *both* directions: the study of the structure and functioning of the personality as a system, in relation to other personalities; and the study of the functioning of the social system as a system. (Parsons, 1964, p. 20)

Parsons restates his explicit anti-reductionism which insists on the action frame of reference of three systems of action. The problem with Durkheim and other sociologists is that in concentrating on the social system as a system they have failed 'to consider systematically the implications of the fact that it is the *interaction of personalities* which constitutes the social system . . . and that, therefore, adequate analysis of motivational process in such a system must reckon with the problems of personality'. On the other hand, Freud and his followers 'by concentrating on the single personality, have failed to consider adequately the implications of the individual's interaction with other personalities *to form a system*' (p. 20). For Parsons the social system is not reducible to personality because it is constituted by the interaction of personalities.

This system of interaction is central to the notion of socialization and in it is constituted the process of internalization. Interacting persons are to be conceived to be objects to each other in two respects. Firstly, they are objects to the person in the sense of cognitive perception and conceptualization, and secondly, in terms of 'meaning' in an emotional sense, that is, they are *cathectic* objects. Freud used the term cathexis (*Besetzung*) to describe the quantity of energy attaching to any object-representation. Object-cathexis refers to energy (in Parsons' terms 'meaning', i.e., of attachment or aversion) invested in external objects. Thirdly, a person is said to orient himself to an object by evaluation, i.e. the integration of cognitive and cathectic meanings of the object to form a system. Parsons maintains that 'no stable relation between two or more objects is possible without all three modes of orientation being present for both parties to the relationship' (p. 21).

Now, the condition on which such stability depends is the existence of *common culture*. That is, a commonly shared system of symbols whose meanings are commonly understood. Such a system is common to every known society and especially, but not exclusively, it involves language. The precise articulation of the concepts of culture and of language in sociological and anthropological theories differ in detail from one account to another. Arguing as much in *The Social System*, Parsons writes that 'in anthropological theory there is not what could be called close agreement on the definition of the concept of culture' (p. 15). He nevertheless ventures to pick out what he calls 'three prominant keynotes'. Culture is transmitted, learned and shared, and further, 'culture is on the one hand the product of, on the other a determinant of systems of human social interaction' (p. 15). For Parsons language is a functionally essential aspect of culture and of social systems: 'a social system (in the present sense) is not possible without language, and without other minimum patterns of culture' (p. 35). Language is a functional prerequisite of social systems, but by no means the only functional prerequisite. Culture is said to be both a product and a determinant of social systems but the circularity of the designation of culture and the combination of the concept of culture with the notion of it as a functional prerequisite leads to fundamental theoretical problems for Parsons' work. His remark that '*however* the going symbol systems of the society may have developed in the first place, they are involved in the socialization of every child' masks these problems but it cannot hide them, as we shall see.

For Parsons both the cathectic and the cognitive images of persons relative to each other are functions of their interaction in the system of social relations. Thus a 'social system is a function of common culture, which not only forms the basis of the intercommunication of its members, but which defines, and so in one sense determines, the relative statuses of its members' and there is 'no intrinsic significance of persons to each other independent of their actual interaction' (p. 22). Common culture defines and regulates these relative statuses so that 'what persons *are* can only be understood in terms of a set of beliefs and sentiments which define what they *ought to be*' (p. 22). Thus for Parsons the process of socialization and its mechanism, the process of internalization, is dependent upon a level of culture external to interaction, external to the social system, in which basic categories of what 'ought to be' are located. We need not speculate what this level of culture represents because Parsons himself refers to it as 'ultimate reality'.[12] Ultimate reality, which is synonymous with religious beliefs, provides the basic categories of meaning which direct action in general. They establish what 'ought' to be.

The religious character of Parsons' notion of ultimate reality apart, what is significant is that if the process with which we are concerned (i.e., the process of socialization, its mechanism of internalization, and the role of culture) is indeed dependent upon a level of 'cultural reality' which is external to social systems it cannot be the product of social systems. Despite these problems Parsons proceeds to attach central theoretical significance to total common culture and indeed the 'place of the superego as part of the structure of the personality must be understood in terms of the *relation* between personality and the total common culture' (p. 23).

For Parsons, Freud's view of the superego was too narrow in that 'the inescapable conclusion is that not only moral standards, but *all components of the common culture* are internalized as part of the personality structure' (p. 23). The content of both cathectic-attitudes and cognitive-status definitions have cultural significance and this content is *cultural and learned*. Freud

> failed to take explicity into account the fact that the frame of reference in terms of which objects are cognized, and therefore adapted to, is cultural and thus cannot be taken for granted as given, but must be internalized as a condition of the development of mature ego-functioning. In this respect it seems to be correct to say that Freud introduced an unreal separation between the superego and the ego—the lines between them are in fact difficult to define in his theory. (p. 23)

Parsons' conclusions are that the distinction which Freud makes between the superego and the ego, that the former is internalized, by identification, whilst the latter consists of responses to external reality (external to the human individual that is) rather than of internalized culture, is not tenable. Parsons argues that: 'these responses are, to be sure, *learned* responses; but internalization is a very special kind of learning which Freud seemed to confine to the superego' (p. 24). We are not concerned, here, with Parsons' reading of Freud who 'did not appreciate the presence and significance of a common culture of expressive-affective symbolism', but with Parsons' own conceptualization of the internalization of common culture.

For Parsons, the crucial problem concerns the process of internalization of common culture, including all three of its major components—the cognitive reference system, the system of expressive symbolism, and the system of moral standards. Internalization is constituted by what Parsons calls 'integration with affect'. Culture is a system of generalized symbols and their meanings. For internalization to take place the individual's own affective organization must achieve levels of generalization of a high order and this is achieved by the building up of attachments to other persons by emotional communication with others so that the individual is sensitized to the attitudes of others. Now, the process of forming attachments is in itself inherently a process of generalization of affect and this generalization is in a 'major aspect the process of symbolization of emotional meanings—that is, it is a process of the acquisition of culture' (p. 29).

Here we have it then. Cathexis of an object (other individuals, cultural objects etc.) is the focal point for the development of *motivation* for the internalization of cultural patterns. Nevertheless, the problem of the location of certain evaluative elements of culture in a sphere of 'ultimate reality' remains. We have the mechanisms of the process of socialization but on the condition that the means of differentiation in the process of socialization, a central issue in the dual problem, remains at a level beyond theorization, in the realm of ultimate reality.

Now it might be supposed that the *conditions* of socialization are crucial to the process, to differentiation and to educational achievement. Indeed, this is just what is argued by sociologists of education. However, for Parsons, in 'The School Class as a Social System' differential *material* conditions of socialization cannot be the source of further and wider differentiation because 'except for sex in certain respects, there is no formal basis for differentiation of status within the school class' (pp. 437–8). We will return in more detail to the question of differentiation presently. Parsons is concerned with 'conditions of socialization' in a quite different context, for,

The conditions of socialization of a person are such that the gratifications which derive from his cathexis of objects cannot be secured unless, along with generalization of emotional meanings and their communication, he also develops a cognitive categorization of objects, including himself, and a system of moral norms which regulate the relations between himself and the object (a superego). (Parsons, 1964, p. 29)

Parsons argues that this clarifies a confusion in Freud's method. He also argues that Freud 'denies that the very young child is capable of object cathexis, and speaks of identification, in contrast with object cathexis, as "the earliest form of emotional tie with an object"' (p. 30). Whilst Parsons agrees that the child's early attachment to the mother and his latter cathexis of her are not the same thing, he argues that,

> It seems probable that the earliest attachment is, as it were, precultural, while true object cathexis involves the internalization of a cultural symbol system. (Parsons, 1964, p. 30)

There are clearly some problems with Parsons' formulations. Firstly, his separation of the 'precultural' from 'true object cathexis' involving the cultural system is no less arbitrary than his critique of Freud's 'unreal separation between the superego and the ego'. That is, Parsons establishes no rigorous theoretical means of separation. His concept of internalization resorts ultimately to a speculative philosophical anthropology.

Parsons invokes the notion of *pre-given* capacities on the part of the biological organism to respond adequately to the cultural realm. The process of socialization, which is central to Parsons' sociological theory of education, involves the process of the 'learning of value orientations'. It is not until the human individual is taught or has learned to respond to values that he is 'human'. It is only then that he can become an organized individual (fulfill the requirements of the personality system) and a social actor (become integrated into the social system). However, for Parsons this capacity is already presupposed and the organism is designed so as to allow the development of the value–orientational components of action. The notion of the 'plasticity' of the human organism in allowing the determinate intervention of values is central to his thesis:

> We have already said that the way is cleared for value standards to be effective whenever the plasticity of the organism leaves the realm of freedom in the relation between the situation and the organism and we have said that value standards are involved in the *evaluative mode* of motivational orientation as rules and recipes for guiding selections. (Parsons and Shils, 1962)

The human organism is provided with a *pre-given* capacity to respond to value orientations. Thus, the organism is *always already* a subject and the process by which the ego is 'constituted' is merely the realization of that which is already present in the organism. Parsons does not provide a theory by which the ego is formed but operates with an ambiguous circularity. The learning process is not a mechanism by which the personality is formed but a process of the realization of an immanent capacity of the 'precultural' 'human' biological organism. On the other hand, the values involved in the process are located in a realm of ultimate reality.

## (ii) DIFFERENTIATION

Internalization and differentiation are components of a 'dual problem' and these components are not empirically separable, nor are they theoretically separable in the structural functionalist theory of the functions of the school class.

Much of the sociology of education revolves around discussion of the mechanisms of the reproduction of the socio-technical division of labour. Parsons sees these mechanisms as largely operative in the school class but considers other agencies such as the family to be of functional importance, as are informal peer groups, churches, voluntary organizations and 'on-the-job' training. The mechanisms of the reproduction of the socio-technical division of labour are dependent upon the mechanisms of differentiation of individuals. The latter is intrinsically tied up with the mechanisms of internalization: this tie up is the 'dual problem'.

Parsons sets out in 'The School Class as a Social System' to analyse the particular mechanisms, operative in the school class, which secure differentiation and allocation of individuals to occupational roles in adult society and their concomitant value orientations. There is no teleology here, in the sense that there is no necessity that the dual problem is satisfied. Quite simply, if certain conditions on which stable interaction depends are not satisfied then society cannot exist. One of these conditions is the stabilizing action of common culture and its transmission from generation to generation. The particular mechanism operative in the school class is the 'selective process' which Parsons considers is,

> genuinely assortive. As in virtually all comparable processes, ascriptive as well as achieved factors influence the outcome. In this case, the ascriptive factor is the socio-economic status of the child's family, and the factor underlying his opportunity for achievement is his individual ability. (Parsons, 1964, pp. 131–2)

Now, it is important to note here that 'socio-economic status' does not refer to, or indicate, any differential ability on the part of the child's family to secure on his behalf privileged access to educational resources. It is merely 'an indication of father's occupation' which is seen to ascribe particular achievement orientation. Parsons thus considers that the main selection process takes place 'on a single main axis of achievement' which is prescribed by particular family value orientation, together with 'individual ability'. The dual selection/socialization process leads gradually via the process of differentiation to the allocation of occupational roles in the adult society and to the internalization of concomitant value orientations. For Parsons it is essentially value orientation (underlined by ability) which determines selection and allocation and its necessary and concomitant value orientations.

The common value orientation to which the child's family, his school class and society all subscribe is that of achievement, and although Parsons sees 'cause for strain' through differential rewards for achievers and non-achievers, 'this common valuation helps to make possible the acceptance of the crucial differentiation, especially by the losers in the competition' (ibid., p. 145) 'the valuation of achievement and its sharing by family and school not only provides the appropriate values for internalization by individuals, but also performs a crucial integrative function for the system' (ibid., p. 145). So, whilst differential value orientation towards achievement is necessary for, and leads ultimately to, differential role allocation in the adult society and thus differential concomitant value orientation, the commitment of all to the common value of achievement performs the function of the integrative mechanism of society. The school class as a social system functions to allocate manpower 'required by society' and to secure the necessary and 'correct' intersubjective relations between, and specific techniques in, differentiated social actors.

Culture plays a crucial role in the dual problem in that it constitutes the content in the process of internalization/socialization so that value orientations (e.g. achievement motivation) secure *both* the integration of society and the differentiation of social roles and their acceptance by social actors. We have, however, already noted some problems in Parsons' concept of culture and the relations between the cultural system and the other systems. Parsons' most explicit comments on the cultural system appear in his later work, *Societies: Evolutionary and Comparative Perspectives*. Here it is argued that the central functional exigency of the interrelations between a society and a cultural system is the legitimation of the society's normative order. For Parsons the school class is one of the agencies functioning to legitimate that order via the processes by which differentiation is made acceptable.

Cultural value patterns provide the most direct link between the social and cultural systems in legitimizing the normative order of the society. The core of a society as a social system is the patterned normative order through which the life of a population is collectively organized. As an order it *contains* values and differentiated and particularized norms and rules, all of which require cultural references in order to be meaningful and legitimate. The cultural system structures commitments vis-à-vis ultimate reality into meaningful orientations towards the rest of the environment and the system of action, the physical world, organisms, personalities and social systems. The origin and determination of cultural values resides with a sphere of ultimate reality which structures orientations and gives them meaning. For Parsons ultimate reality is an

> . . . environment above action—the 'ultimate reality' with which we are ultimately concerned in grappling with what Weber called the 'problems of meaning'—e.g., evil and suffering, the temporal limitations of human life, and the like. 'Ideas' in this area, as cultural objects, are in some sense symbolic 'representations' (e.g., concepts of gods, totems, the supernatural) of the ultimate realities, but are not themselves such realities. (Parsons, 1966, p. 8)

Thus the common culture and the value orientations which derive from it are situated in a realm which is beyond investigation—a sphere of ultimate reality. The process of internalization, which constitutes the concept of socialization, and the process of differentiation which is dependent on differentiated value orientation and 'meanings' are theoretically dependent upon the existence of a realm which is beyond theorization. The functions of the school class as a social system are empirically delineated but without coherent theoretical foundation in that the means of organization of its functions are effects of a sphere which lies outside the realm of possible theorization.


## C. BRITISH SOCIOLOGY OF EDUCATION

If the traditional sociology of education derives from Durkheim and from structural-functionalism, then not only is it outweighed in theoretical sophistication by its foundations but it also carries many theoretical problems. In particular the concept of culture and its relation to the processes within the educational system remain problematic. However, there is a sense in which it is not accurate to say that the sociology of education in Britain is based on Durkheim and structural-functionalism. There is, to be sure, a 'strand' of sociology of education in which the terms of reference are so derived. There is, however, also a strand which is based on what is known as demographic 'class' analysis and there is a third strand which, in attempting to account for the results of the demographic analysis, combines material and cultural explanations and in so doing revives many of the problems that we have seen to be associated with structural-functionalism.

We have seen that Parsons' account of the functions of education is derived from a level of analysis of the school class as a system of interaction. Now, to some extent the sociology of education in Britain abandoned this level of analysis in that it was concerned with differentials in educational opportunity and achievement between social classes.[13] A brief comment is necessary here on the concept of classes used in contemporary sociology of education.

Much of the empirical research in the sociology of education and the collection of data for use in government reports on education uses neither a sociological nor a Marxist conception of class but, rather, the Registrar-General's categories.[14] Many sociologists of education and Marxists use these categories. In addition it is common to find classes distinguished simply in terms of income or disposable income. The point here is that access to educational resources for children can be largely influenced by the level of disposable income of their parents. The distribution of income has been subject to considerable scrutiny in recent years and it is not necessary to reproduce the results here. However, an illustration of the privileged access to income from investment and earnings can be seen in Table 1.1 and Figure 1.1, which are taken from the *Royal Commission on the Distribution of Income and Wealth*, Cmnd. 6171 (The Diamond Report, 1975). The privileged access to both investment income and higher levels of earned income affords privileged access to educational resources for the children of the middle and upper classes.

Since access to educational resources, like access to medical and legal resources is subject to financial criteria at the level of individual person, many critics of the education system have argued, correctly, that the notion of 'equality of educational opportunity' is a sham. On the other hand, against this argument there are the cultural arguments about inequality of educational achievement between social classes. In a sense these cultural arguments have taken the place of the old, discredited arguments on IQ but many of the problems remain. For just as there is no means of determining the relative importance of alleged 'intelligence' against other factors such as the financial privilege/barriers to access, neither is there any means by which the relative importance of 'cultural determinants' can be determined.[15]

Over the last three decades British sociology of education has been concerned with the process of socialization of human individuals, and with the social class differentials in educational opportunity and achievement. These two issues are interrelated in that differences in the conditions and the process of socialization are used to account for the social class differentials in educational achievement. The conditions in and through which the socialization process occurs are composed of both a material and a cultural sphere. The social institutions of the family and the educational system which are the main agents of socialization are composed, like other social institutions, of these spheres or realms. The sociology of education is concerned with four major elements and with relations between them: the cultural resources of the family, the cultural resources of the school, the material resources of the family and the material resources of the school. In addition there is usually some reference to the cultural and material resources of the 'community' which usually includes whatever is excluded by the other categories. For example, in communities where employers are able to keep wages low there are material effects on families, their children and consequently on their education. In communities where routine maintenance is not carried out there are consequences for the health and general well-being of families, their children and their education.

Overarching these categories is the conception of class differentials and there is considerable demographic evidence that the social class *differentials* in educational achievement[16] have changed little during this century despite the considerable attention of educational policy to questions of access and forms of organization of education, in particular with reference to the 'working class'. A range of factors have been proposed and have competed for consideration as governing the patterns and constituting the conditions of social class differentials in educational achievement. Factors such as personality structure (individual 'intelligence', motivation, etc.), culture (shared norms, values, beliefs, etc.), and material social conditions (of schools, homes, communities), have been proposed and considered. An earlier dominance of psychological explanation of the educational achievement of groups of *individuals* in terms of alleged attributes of personality structure, namely 'intelligence', has been overtaken by predominantly sociological explanation of social class differentials in terms of material and cultural conditions of socialization and education.

The sociology of education in Britain established itself largely on the force of the argument that social rather than psychological explanation was the appropriate explanation for the social character of patterns of educational achievement. Indeed these arguments were largely instrumental, together with the political power of certain sections of the Labour Party, in the breaking of the stranglehold of psychometric testing as a major instrument

TABLE 1.1 Distribution of personal income

Percentage shares of income, before and after income tax, received by given quantile groups; 1949 to 1972/73

United Kingdom                                                               Income unit: tax unit

| Quantile group | Before income tax | | | | | Income range 1972/73 (lower limit) | After income tax | | | | | Income range 1972/73 (lower limit) |
|---|---|---|---|---|---|---|---|---|---|---|---|---|
| | 1949 % | 1959 % | 1964 % | 1967 % | 1972/73 % | £ p.a. | 1949 % | 1959 % | 1964 % | 1967 % | 1972/73 % | £ p.a. |
| Top 1 per cent | 11.2 | 8.4 | 8.2 | 7.4 | 6.4 | 6,236 | 6.4 | 5.3 | 5.3 | 4.9 | 4.4 | 4,462 |
| 2–5 ,, ,, | 12.6 | 11.5 | 11.3 | 11.0 | 10.8 | 3,512 | 11.3 | 10.5 | 10.7 | 9.9 | 9.8 | 2,853 |
| 6–10 ,, ,, | 9.4 | 9.5 | 9.6 | 9.6 | 9.7 | 2,857 | 9.4 | 9.4 | 9.9 | 9.5 | 9.4 | 2,398 |
| Top 10 per cent | 33.2 | 29.4 | 29.1 | 28.0 | 26.9 | 2,857 | 27.1 | 25.2 | 25.9 | 24.3 | 23.6 | 2,398 |
| 11–20 ,, ,, | 14.1 | 15.1 | 15.5 | 15.2 | 15.8 | 2,289 | 14.5 | 15.7 | 16.1 | 15.2 | 15.8 | 1,988 |
| 21–30 ,, ,, | 11.2 | 12.6 | 12.6 | 12.6 | 13.1 | 1,937 | 11.9 | 12.9 | 12.9 | 13.0 | 13.2 | 1,679 |
| 31–40 ,, ,, | 9.6 | 10.7 | 10.9 | 11.1 | 11.0 | 1,626 | 10.5 | 11.2 | 11.1 | 11.0 | 11.2 | 1,421 |
| 41–50 ,, ,, | 8.2 | 9.1 | 9.2 | 9.1 | 9.2 | 1,338 | 9.5 | 9.9 | 8.8 | 9.7 | 9.5 | 1,187 |
| 51–60 ,, ,, | } 23.7 | 7.5 | 7.4 | 7.7 | 7.5 | 1,065 | } 26.5 | 7.2 | 8.0 | 7.7 | 8.0 | 978 |
| 61–70 ,, ,, | | 5.9 | 5.8 | 6.0 | 5.2 | 837 | | 6.6 | 5.6 | 7.1 | 6.5 | 801 |
| 71–80 ,, ,, | | 4.4 | 4.3 | 4.8 | 4.8 | 644 | | 5.2 | 5.1 | 4.9 | 5.5 | 637 |
| 81–90 ,, ,, | | } 5.3 | } 5.2 | 3.4 | } 5.8 | — | | } 6.0 | } 6.5 | } 7.1 | } 6.8 | — |
| 91–100 ,, ,, | | | | 2.2 | | | | | | | | |
| Differences as a percentage of the median between: upper and lower quantile | — | 98 | 103 | 91 | 101 | | — | 98 | 105 | 90 | 92 | |

| Median | £ p.a. | £259 | £514 | £679 | £843 | £1,338 | £250 | £477 | £596 | £758 | £1,187 |
|---|---|---|---|---|---|---|---|---|---|---|---|
| Gini coefficient | % | 41.1 | 39.8 | 39.9 | 38.2 | 37.4 | 35.5 | 36.0 | 36.6 | 33.5 | 33.1 |

*Source:* pre 1972/73 figures derived from Blue Book: 1972/73 figures derived from provisional CSO income distribution table.

*Note:* In some years the income share of the lower quantile groups cannot be estimated with any degree of confidence as the published range tables have too few income ranges at the lower end of the distribution to permit successful interpolation.

*Source: Royal Commission on the Distribution of Income and Wealth*, Report No. 1, 1975, Cmnd. 6171, (Diamond Report), Table 15, p. 45.

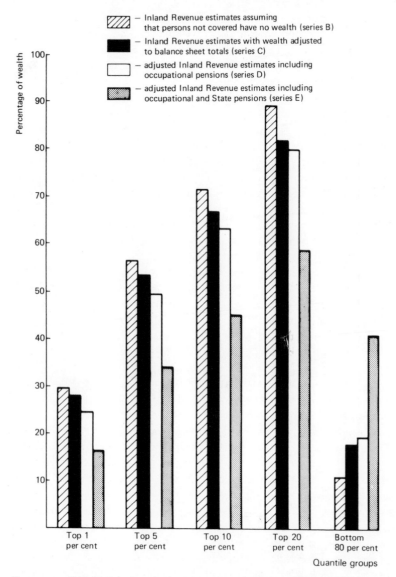

FIGURE I.I *Distribution of personal wealth in Great Britain on alternative bases; 1972*

Alternative estimates of the percentage shares of personal wealth owned by given quantile groups of the total population aged 18 and over

*Source*: *Royal Commission on the Distribution of Income and Wealth*, Report No. I. 1975, Cmnd. 6171, Diamond Report, p. 144, figure 14, which is derived from Tables 34 and 39 of the same report.

in the allocation of educational resources and in promoting the moves towards the reorganization of secondary education on non-selective lines. The sociology of education established that the distribution of resources themselves was a major source of differential educational achievement between the classes.

## (i) LANGUAGE AND THE SOCIOLOGY OF EDUCATION

One of the most common components of the cultural argument in the explanation of social class differentials in educational achievement is that of the role of language. We have already seen that for Parsons language is an important aspect of culture. In British sociology of education the work of Basil Bernstein, much of which has now been collected together in the volumes of his *Class, Codes and Control*, has been prominent in accounting for the importance of language in socialization and education. Bernstein has argued that linguistic 'codes' developed by children during their primary socialization, and specifically in relationships with the mother, differ between when he calls the 'working class' and the 'middle class'. We shall return to Bernstein's conception of 'class' presently.

Bernstein's studies are concerned with childrens' *forms* of speech; not with dialect nor with matters of underlying grammar or with slang but with the different *use* of vocabulary and the grammatical system. The differences arise from the 'social structure' and, specifically, out of different forms and techniques of socialization. Bernstein argues that working class children develop forms of speech which are typified by a 'restricted code' as an effect of primary socialization in which the mother places (in comparison to the 'ideal type' middle class mother) 'less emphasis upon language when she controls her child and deals with only the particular act and does not relate it to general principles and their reasoned basis and consequences' (Bernstein, 1971, p. 220). The forms of speech thus generated are typified by the *restricted* code in the sense that there is a 'restriction on the *contexts* and on the *conditions* which will orient the child to universalistic orders of meanings and to making those linguistic choices through which such meanings are realised and so made public' (ibid., p. 197). Middle class children on the other hand are alleged to develop an 'elaborated code' which Bernstein designates as the conceptual opposite to the restricted code. The elaborated code is the product of forms and techniques of socialization which are in exact opposition to those used by working class mothers.

The differences thus generated become crucial when the child enters school because the linguistic form adopted by the school is that of the elaborated code. Thus the middle class child is already familier with the forms of language used in the school whilst the working class child, Bernstein argues, has first to learn how to learn. That is, in order to learn he must first learn the elaborated code in which school work is expressed.

Bernstein's work has been used to account for social class differentials in educational achievement in terms of differences in 'educability'. Working class children have been said to be lingustically and/or culturally deprived and as such (in comparison to middle class children) less 'educable'. Bernstein has resisted such interpretations of his work as 'misinterpretations'. However, it is clear that his work (which now spreads over two decades) does not constitute a unitary discourse governed by a principle of coherence. Appearing within it are positions which are contradictory, and in particular, earlier arguments which Bernstein, with good reason, wishes to displace. Thus, some of the interpretations of his work which he designates 'misinterpretations' may well be legitimate, even though they are representations of positions which he now rejects.

An examination here of Bernstein's work over the last two decades[17] is, of course, quite out of the question. Rather, I will examine here a partitular aspect of Bernstein's work on language and culture with which he too has been particularly concerned; the *consequences* of his work for educational policy and for pedagogic practice. This is an area in which Bernstein claims to have been misunderstood and in which he has been at pains to 'reinterpret' the meaning of his research findings.

Bernstein addresses the consequences of his work in a short paper first published under the title 'A Critique of the Concept of "Compensatory Education"' in the book *Education for Democracy*.[18] The editors of that book conceived the collection of articles in it as expressing some of the ideas embraced by the notion of 'progressive education', and as such a response to the Black Papers.[19] The editors of *Education for Democracy* suggested that the ideas of the progressives had 'gained adherents right across the political spectrum' (Rubinstein and Stoneman, 1970, p. 9) although clearly not amongst the right-wing supporters of the Black Papers. The editors of *Education for Democracy* argued that the high degree of unanimity with which its contributors spoke was 'due to the logical coherence of the progressive view of education' which was 'in sharp contrast to the many, often conflicting positions of the traditionalists, as manifested in the Black Papers' (ibid., p. 9). In contributing to the collection in *Education for Democracy* Bernstein is forced to confront the *political* consequences of his discourse in a double sense; in the sense of its consequences for educational policy and in the sense of its consequences for his political allegiance (to the progressives and their leftist associations as against the traditionalists and their rightist political associations).

In his article Bernstein gives a short account of his work on linguistic codes and is concerned to counter what he argues are misrepresentations of his position. The explicit aim of the paper is to attack the *concept* of 'compensatory education'. Referring to the evidence of the *Newsom Report*[20] on the gross material inadequacy of certain schools Bernstein argues,

> I do not understand how we can talk about offering compensatory education to children who in the first place have not, as yet, been offered an adequate educational environment. (Bernstein, 1970, p. 111)

Bernstein is against the *concept* of compensatory education; against the *idea* that any provision of an adequate educational environment, where none had been provided before, could be considered as 'compensatory' whether it formed part of a compensatory programme or not. Bernstein is not against the provision furnished by educational programmes called 'compensatory'.

With respect to the concepts of culture and language Bernstein rejects as a misinterpretation the equating of his concept of 'restricted code' with the notion of 'linguistic' or 'cultural deprivation'. He argues further that the notion of the teaching of the 'elaborated code' has become part of the concept of the provision of compensatory education, but that contrary to such a notion the teaching of children to use the elaborated code is not *compensatory* education; it *is* education. He suggests that: 'we should stop thinking in terms of 'compensatory education' but consider instead, most seriously and systematically the conditions and the contexts of the educational environment' (ibid., p. 114). Bernstein is at pains to displace the concepts of 'compensatory education', and the related concepts of 'cultural deprivation', 'linguistic deprivation' and 'social disadvantage' because as he says,

> the work I have been doing has inadvertently contributed towards their formulation. It might, and has been said, that my research through focusing upon the subculture and forms of familial socialization has also distracted attention from the conditions and contexts of learning in schools. (ibid., p. 144)

On the question of linguistic codes he recognises that 'the concept "restricted code" has been equated with "linguistic deprivation" or even the non-verbal child' (ibid., p. 144) but in terms of his research formulations he gives very little ground, maintaining that working class mothers are not 'non-verbal' but nevertheless that they: 'differ from the middle class mothers in the *contexts* which evoke universalistic meanings. They are *not* linguistically de-prived, neither are their children (ibid., p. 177; emphasis in the original).

Bernstein thus attempts both to maintain his theoretical argument on the generation of linguistic codes (in particular, here, the argument that working class socialization and culture generates the restricted code), and to align himself with Left progressives who do not regard linguistic and cultural differences as the *cause* of social and educational inequalities. Bernstein first unites with them in their insistence that social inequality and the lack of provision of an adequate *educational* environment for certain groups of children is largely responsible for their lack of educational achievement and the subsequent social class differentials. He agrees that his work on socialization has drawn attention away from these dominantly important issues only to then revert to his theory of socialization and linguistic codes. Bernstein wants to have it both ways, or, as Harold Rosen has put it in his article 'Language and Class', 'as the Jewish proverb has it, he is trying to dance at two weddings at the same time'.[21]

What Bernstein argues in effect is that working class children *are* deprived of the ability to use the elaborated code as a result of their socialization and that the teaching of children to be able to utilize the elaborated code is not compensatory education.

> The introduction of the child to the universalistic meanings of public forms of thought is not compensatory education; *it is* education. It is not making children middle class . . . (Bernstein, 1970, p. 120)

Now there are clearly a number of serious problems here Firstly, Bernstein correctly argues that the use of the elaborated code and the invoking of universalistic meanings is not a middle class preserve (whatever that might mean). We could add that neither is literacy in general, nor is numeracy. Nevertheless, Bernstein conceives of the working class child as a deficit system, deprived of something (elaborated code) that middle class children are alleged to have as a result of their socialization. In fact, Bernstein's concept of the restricted code is no concept at all; it represents merely an alleged *absence* of something alleged to be found in middle class children. Hence the curiously exact opposites of the elaborated and the restricted codes. We will come to Bernstein's conception of classes and their alleged attributes very shortly.

For the moment it should be noted that, the theory of codes apart, Bernstein's comments on educational provision and the consequences for educational policy and for pedagogic practice are quite sound. Bernstein arrives at a position in which he argues that the proper role of the educational system is to take whatever capacities children have and to use them as a starting point but to go on to develop and extend them. The educational system rather than the family, *here*,[22] is the major social institution with responsibility for education. The creation of an adequate educational environment is the priority of *schools* and responsibility cannot be displaced onto the home. Bernstein's position is distinct from that of the radicals who treat working class culture as an end in itself, and it is also distinct from that of those traditionalists who treat the school as an agency with the hopeless task of combating the effects of working class culture. Bernstein's adoption of a position in opposition to this latter position is clearly incompatible with his theory of codes.

One of the main sources of the theoretical problems in Bernstein's work is in his conception of 'class' and in his attempts to associate forms of socialization, language and codes with classes. Despite the appearance of the *word* class in many of the papers and in the title of his collection of papers *Class, Codes and Control*, Bernstein has no coherent, and certainly no elaborated conception of 'class'. As Harold Rosen and others have pointed out, we are provided with a conception of class only by implication. Bernstein's class system consists merely of a 'working class' and a 'middle class'. The latter is populated by mothers who are articulate, skilled child minders whilst the former is not. The working class, like the middle class, has no internal differentiation in Bernstein's conception. The concepts of class, like the concepts of codes developed upon them, are nothing but dichotomous oppositions.

In his earlier research, on which the notion of restricted and elaborated codes is based, it is observed that certain groups of 'working class' and of 'middle class' mothers use childrearing techniques which are different in the *use* of language and in the form of language used. Now, no adequate means is provided to demonstrate that these groups were representative of the working class or the middle class in the generality of the concepts of class that Bernstein infers them to represent. There is, therefore, no means of determining that certain uses of language in socialization and certain forms of linguistic code are generated through such forms of socialization in specific classes in general in the way Bernstein infers. Thus, the 'restricted code' and the 'elaborated code' are designated as 'types' or 'ideal types' by Bernstein himself. Given the lack of theoretical and empirical rigour in which these 'ideal types' were formulated there is little or no reason to treat them as anything but *stereotypes*. The theory of codes depends on stereotypes in a double sense. Stereotypes of linguistic codes are implied from and implied to stereotypes of social classes. The consequences for educational policy and for pedagogic practice based on Bernstein's theory of codes are obvious. If 'working class' children are essentially less 'educable' than their 'middle class' opposites, then no amount of change in policy or practice could alter the patterns of social class differentials in educational achievement.

In his paper 'A Critique of the Concept of "Compensatory Education"' Bernstein is unable to *combine* his theory of codes with the progressive comments he makes on educational provision except at a superficial level. On the contrary there are two discrete levels of discourse; the theory of codes and the commentary on provision. Bernstein's comments on provision cannot be deduced from his theory of codes. The consequences of his commentary for educational policy and for pedagogic practice (unlike the consequences of his theory of codes) are progressive. Bernstein's work, however, does not provide any indication of the means of achieving such progress.

## (ii) CLASS, CULTURE AND EDUCATION

We have already noted that in British sociology of education the concept of 'class' has particular significance. The concept is used to describe differentials in educational opportunity and achievement, usually between the 'working class' and the 'middle class'. We have already noted that in various accounts these differentials are attributed to differential access to cultural and material resources, or some combination of these. Two theoretical problems have been discussed so far. On the one hand the theoretical problem of conceptualization of culture and on the other its relations with other aspects of social structure. These problems and the absence of rigorous solution to them leaves the account of the conditions of existence of class differentials in educational achievement problematic. The differentials, however, remain, as do the differentials in access to educational opportunity via differentials in levels of disposable income.

Now, much of the sociology of education is concerned with a critique of inequality of educational opportunity between the classes. Writers, including sociologists as well as the authors of Government reports, have insisted that many factors are important to the provision of an adequate educational environment, and in their conclusions resort to some combination of differences in material resources and differences in culture in explanation of differences in educational achievement between social classes. The debate over the relative importance of the social institutions of the family and the educational system is combined with debate over the relative importance of culture and material resources. Influential writers such as Jackson and Marsden in their classic *Education and the Working Class* and J. W. B. Douglas in his equally renowned *The Home and the School*, as well as many other authors, explain differences in educational achievement between social classes in terms of both culture and material resources. For such writers, to resort to the realm of culture, to the realm in particular of values, attitudes and personality structure, in addition to material resources, leaves unresolved the problem of the precise determination of such values, attitudes and personality structure, and the mode of their effectivity.

Let us take an element of the cultural argument in order to illustrate this difficulty. By way of an example let us take the very common argument which alleges that the educational achievement of working class children is relatively inferior to that of middle class children because of the 'lack of interest' of working class parents in their childrens' education.

A commonly used index of parental interest in the education of their children which is used both by teachers and by sociologists of education is the frequency of parental attendance at formal and informal parent-teacher meetings and similar events. It is evident from many accounts that parents of working class children, and particularly their fathers, are underrepresented at such meetings in comparison with middle and lower middle class parents. It is concluded that in comparison with middle class parents working class parents lack interest in the children's education. This alleged lack of interest is then used to account, at least in part, for the relative underachievement of working class children.

Now, non-communication between parents and teachers may well cause certain difficulties and communication clearly is to be encouraged. However, what is being argued is not that there are difficulties caused by lack of communication but that certain attitudes of working class parents result in the relative underachievement of their children. Cultural differences, differences in attitudes, values etc. between the home and the school are alleged to be a major obstacle to working class educational achievement. The 'evidence' for such differences is the manifest behaviour of parents. It is to this manifest behaviour that meaning is imputed by teachers, educationalists and sociologists. Their conclusion that working class parents lack interest in their children's education is no more than speculation. Furthermore, if differences in values, attitudes, 'interest' etc. cannot be determined other than by speculation, neither can their mode of effectivity.

The point here is not that there are no differences between the attitudes of middle and working class parents. The point is that the contexts of these differences have to be established and their consequences determined. For example, it is well known that manual workers are often unsympathetic to their children staying at school beyond the statutory leaving age. This occurs in cases where children could indeed benefit from continued schooling. Rather than simply associating lack of educational achievement with working class attitudes the question should be posed as to why particular attitudes persist. Do the attitudes of teachers have anything to do with the attitudes of parents, for example? What can teachers do to improve the educational opportunities of children whose parents are unsympathetic towards education? The reply from teachers might be that if certain parents are unwilling to communicate with them then there is nothing they can do. Such an attitude is, of course, defeatist. Teachers have the advantage over parents in that they are in effective possession of the means of schooling and the knowledge of the workings of the educational system. Democratic moves towards opening the educational system to discussion and debate over policy would encourage parents from many sections of society to participate. A positive attitude on the part of parents could well be developed by sensitive and informative action on the part of teachers. If teachers are concerned with education then it cannot be outside their sphere to involve themselves in informative debate and discussion with the parents of their pupils. What is education if it is not informative debate and discussion?

One of the major differences between middle and working class parents is their access to material resources. Those writers who insist on predominantly cultural explanations of differentials in education achievement between middle and working class children are usually at pains to stress the limitations of a policy which aims to affect (to improve) material resources, and in order to do so designate to the category of material resources a limited sphere which includes little more than bricks and mortar, desks, pencils, blackboards and books. On these grounds it is then argued that the material resources encountered by working class children in schools are no different from the material resources encountered by middle class children, and it is concluded that the crucial factors leading to the differentials in achievement are cultural.

Such an argument rests on the reduction of the category of material resources to physical objects. Of course, the category of material resources includes things such as pupil−teacher ratios, rate of teacher turnover, teacher quality and qualifications in addition to the physical objects already mentioned. The investigation of differences in material conditions is an area of continual theoretical and empirical research. As such research proceeds there is a continued call for forms of intervention and improvement of a whole range of material resources which affect the condition in which children learn. These resources are not restricted to those encountered in formal schooling but include wider resources such as community and housing.

For some writers, however, no such intervention and improvement could overcome the cultural obstacles to education which are alleged to persist. The cultural resources of certain groups of families is said to present an insurmountable obstacle to attempts to improve the educational opportunities of children from certain sections of the working class. Such arguments are still put forward, even today, by such influential writers as John and Elizabeth Newson, who conclude their recent book *Seven Years Old In The Home Environment* with the comment that what they call 'deprived' parents

> will probably produce children who expect nothing and are not equipped to do anything about it. Thus the child born into the lowest social bracket has everything stacked against him *including his parents' principles of child upbringing*. Because we do not see how we can easily change principles which are honestly and firmly held, for this group of children we are pessimistic about the nature of the parental role. (ibid., p. 406; emphasis in the original)

In contrast to these children 'born into the lowest social bracket' the Newsons juxtapose children who 'expect as of right to be privileged and who are very well equipped to realise those expectations' (ibid., p. 406). They are the children of 'privileged parents' who manage to produce such children 'by using the methods that they prefer' (ibid., p. 406).

It is doubtful that the Newsons' extreme 'pessimism' is shared by many sociologists of education. Furthermore, the reduction of privilege and deprivation to expectations and childrearing techniques is absurd. Most writers are, nevertheless, concerned to stress the case for at least the consideration of cultural aspects such as 'expectations', 'values', 'principles', etc., together with the distribution of resources, as the source of differentials in educational achievement. A typical recent example of such a way of thinking by the DES can be found in the document *Higher Education into the 1990s*. Paragraph 32 of that document argues that:

> Recent evidence suggests that youngsters take their decisions about whether or not to aim for higher education well before they reach the age of 18; and that social, cultural and peer-group influences are crucial factors in those decisions. While it may be difficult to point to any particular measures which would have a swift and significant impact on participation by children of manual workers, it is at least possible that

participation by this group will by the 1990s be as much affected by the gathering impact of policies in the fields of housing, health and the social services generally as by educational policies.[23]

This argument reflects the equivocacy of arguments on the conditions of existence of differences in levels of participation in higher education (part of the sociological definition of educational achievement) which are found in the sociology of education and in other discourses on education. Paragraph 32 commences with the suggestion, based on 'recent evidence', that some combination of social, cultural and peer-group influences are crucial factors in the decisions that youths make about whether or not to aim for a higher education. At this stage it seems that the argument is that it is predominantly a cultural problem; a problem of the ideas on which decisions are made, peer-group influences for example. Clearly, this leaves unresolved the issue of the conditions of existence of such ideas, shared cultural norms and values. In addressing themselves to these cultural norms with respect to 'children of manual workers' the authors of the document admit to a difficulty in pointing to measures which would have a swift and significant impact on their participation but, nevertheless, in the very same sentence indicate that it is 'at least possible' that policy changes in the fields of housing, health, social services and educational policy itself might bring about participation.

Now, the issue here is not that there are no cultural conditions at work in influencing the degree of participation. The issue is in the question as to what are the conditions of the alleged cultural norms which are said to govern participation. The DES has the answer to its own question on participation in its suggestion that changes in educational policy itself and in housing and other social policy are the conditions which govern participation. It is clear that changes in opportunity themselves have effects on the ways of thinking about education that predominate in youth culture. That is to say that the issue is not *primarily* a cultural issue at all but an issue of material conditions and circumstances which condition and direct cultural norms and attitudes towards education. These conditions and circumstances are not, of course, restricted to social and educational policy but include economic policy. For example, the existence of occupations in the economy for which higher educational qualifications are a criteria for entry will influence the thinking of youth from all classes on the question of participation in higher education.

(iii)  THE CONCEPT OF CLASS

The use of the concept of class in the sociology of education is the site of one of its greatest strengths but also one of its weaknesses. One of the achievements of the sociology of education has been to expose class differentials to political debate. As we have already noted, sociological evidence has been crucial in the struggle for educational reform and the struggle for working class access to education. The weakness lies in the restriction of educational opportunity to *class* differences.

The use of the concept of class in sociology of education and in educational research generally, involves no agreement on precisely which concept of class is to be used. This is a problem when research 'evidence' which is derived from investigation using one concept of class is used in other accounts where a different conception of class is in currency. Although a major problem arises between different disciplines in educational research there are also problems within sociology of education as such. The concept of class usually adopted in government reports refers to the Registrar-General's categories. However, in sociology there are a number of conceptions of class and none are equivalent to the Registrar-General's occupational categories.

In much educational research either the Registrar-General's categories, or some notion of 'stratum' is adopted, and the 'working class' is often synonymous with manual workers whilst the middle class is synonymous with non-manual professional workers (cf. Bernstein). It is observed that there is a general inequality of distribution of opportunity and attainment of educational qualifications between these classes. Middle and upper middle class children gain more qualifications at school than do working class children and they are therefore more likely to gain access to higher educational qualifications and the professions. Now, whilst this distribution of educational opportunity and achievement along class lines is, in general, beyond dispute, the generality of such an account has certain consequences. Firstly, it obscures other forms of educational inequality of opportunity. More important, however, it obscures the precise levels at which inequality of educational opportunity is administered and thus obscures these levels from political debate. We shall return to this in a moment.

The problems inherent in the generality of the 'class analysis' of contemporary educational opportunity are highlighted in the empirical cases of individuals who do not conform to the general trends. In the past sociologists of education have been able to discount the few working class children who gain higher educational qualifications and access to higher paid occupations and the professions as exceptions to the general trend. They were indeed exceptions and as such they did not challenge the general class theory of educational opportunity and achievement.

In arguing that the generality of the sociological theory of class differentials obscures other forms of inequality of opportunity I do not suggest that there are no class differentials but rather that by investigating the precise character of educational opportunity it is possible to expose the administration of opportunity to wider political debate. Rather than the simplistic notion of class differentials which itself produces a problem of accounting for deviants from the general theory, it is possible to set out a more detailed conceptual framework for the analysis of educational opportunity. Such a framework is not simply a means of production of an analysis but a framework for political activity.

The quality of educational provision in Britain is subject to a number of levels or agencies of direction and to relations between them. The point of problematizing these agencies of direction is that under certain circumstances they could be opened up to wider political debate. They are already arenas of political decision making but at some levels such decisions are shielded from wider democratic debate. The levels or agencies of direction of educational policy in Britain today are as follows: the parliamentary level; the DES and its bodies; the local educational authorities, and in particular the office of Director of Education or Chief Education Officer and relations with the Education Committee;[24] headteacher unions; head teachers of individual schools; teachers' unions; and individual teachers. Now these agencies of direction clearly take different forms. They include individuals such as teachers and headteachers and non-individual agencies such as parliamentary debate and Acts. The force of *none* of these agencies should be discounted or underestimated. Democratically debated decisions at the parliamentary level can be frustrated at present by the actions, not only of headteachers but of individual class teachers. For example, there may be complete agreement at all levels on, say, non-streaming, yet such a policy can be frustrated by the practices of individual teachers. On the other hand, teachers and headteachers are able to initiate practices without reference to other levels or agencies of direction. The point is that the quality of educational provision in Britain is subject to many levels or agencies of direction. This means that differences in quality arise not only between classes, but between individual schools, between local authorities etc. The point is not that they supersede the class differentials in educational opportunity; they supplement them. The sociology of education could make a significant contribution to the political struggle for educational reform by going beyond the generality of class analysis and problematizing the agencies of direction and the relations between them, and by contributing to the struggle for wider democratic debate at the levels of the agencies of direction.[25] We shall return in more detail to these issues in the concluding chapter.

# 2 Radicalism and the New Sociology of Education

In the book *Knowledge and Control*, edited by Michael F. D. Young, and in subsequent publications there emerges a 'new' sociology of education which purports to challenge the traditional sociology of education. The new sociology refers to itself, or is variously described as, the New Directions, the radical, and the phenomenological sociology of education.

The first part of this chapter[1] examines Young's proposals for the sociological investigation of what he conceives as a major focus of political power in society, that is, the organization of educational knowledge. For Young, the political character of educational knowledge is expressed in the nature of its control. Educational knowledge is conceived as a construct of 'underlying meaning', and, as such, a reflection of certain political interests. The task of the New Directions is the exploration of the construction of these meanings, and it is claimed that this can be accomplished by following the 'phenomenological' and philosophical works of Alfred Schutz. In challenging Young's project this chapter is not concerned with any assessment of the political character of education in determinate societies. It is not concerned, for example, with arguments as to whether education in England and Wales, Germany, France or the Soviet Union is political in character. Indeed, rather than making any such assessment, it is demonstrated here that the making of such assessment is impossible in Young's sociological project.

The second part of this chapter examines the claim that the new sociology of education is radical in certain of its characteristics. The consequences of the radical position for educational policy and for pedagogic practice is illustrated by an examination of the work of one of Young's associates, Nell Keddie.[2]

## A. THE 'PHENOMENOLOGICAL' SOCIOLOGY OF THE POLITICS OF EDUCATIONAL KNOWLEDGE

Michael Young's allegation that educational knowledge is necessarily political in character presupposes a specific argument as to the status of knowledge in general. Young posits a conception of what he calls 'science and rationality' and then sets about its demolition. On the site of this demolition he places a conception of the 'sociology of knowledge',[3] which, he argues, is the sociological tool with which the new sociology of education can set about analysing, and can discover, the precise status of educational knowledge. A status to which Young has made speculations which suggest an underlying and necessarily political character.

In the limited conception of 'science' which Young sets up for demolition, science is merely dogma. 'Science and reason' are a 'new absolutism' which 'together with the various social, political and educational beliefs that are assumed to follow from them . . . represent the dominant legitimizing categories' (Young, 1971, p. 3), 'like the feudal, clerical and market dogmas of earlier centuries, the dogmas of rationality and science become open to enquiry' (Young, 1971, p. 3).

We raise no objections, of course, to the attacking of dogma. However, in dogmatically characterizing science and rationality as dogma and then proceeding to attack them for their dogmatism Young is merely attacking his own characterizations and his own dogmatism. Such an operation is, of course, no demolition of science, but Young regards it as sufficient to allow the sociology of knowledge to press its claims, and to reveal knowledge, educational or otherwise, as: 'neither absolute, nor arbitrary, but as "available sets of meanings", which in any context do not merely "emerge", but are collectively "given"' (Young, 1971, p. 3).

It is on these grounds, then, that the new directions for the sociology of education urge sociologists to consider what counts as educational knowledge as problematic. The new sociology of education is therefore no longer conceived as the area of enquiry distinct from the sociology of knowledge, for knowledge is to be considered as a product of social organization. Educational knowledge, like any other knowledge in Young's conception, refers to the shared meanings of human subjects and the criterion for validity of knowledge is intersubjectivity.

> For ordinary discourse, in philosophy or science or everyday communication, or the interactions in a lesson between teacher and pupils, these shared meanings are taken for granted . . . (Young, 1971, p. 5)

The object of the new sociology of education is the exploration of what is 'taken for granted as sets of unquestioned assumptions'. The application of the sociology of knowledge in the new sociology of education enables the sociologist to consider, what counts as education as socially and historically constructed. This process points to an analysis of what are perceived as the dominant definitions of educational knowledge by different groups at particular times. This takes us back to the *political nature* of education . . . (Young, 1972, p. 202; emphasis added)

Young thus asserts his position concerning the value of the sociology of knowledge, in which discourses in science, philosophy and everyday communication alike, become subject to *sociological* analysis on the grounds that they are nothing but shared subjective meanings, socially and historically constructed. It is this extreme relativism and subjectivism which has occasioned the critical response[4] to his assertions which, as we shall see, Young attempts to deflect by adopting a tactic in which he reveals the character of his 'radicalism' and the nature of his new directions for the sociology of education.[5] For the moment, however, we will restrict ourselves to an examination of his elaboration of the mechanisms in which the necessarily political character of educational knowledge is revealed.

(i)  THE POLITICS OF EDUCATIONAL KNOWLEDGE

In the paper, *On the Politics of Educational Knowledge*, Young argues that the major fault to be found in previous analyses of the politics of educational knowledge, of which Manzer's book entitled *Teachers and Politics* is exemplary, is the failure to consider conflicts of meaning. Young argues that in Manzer's work, what counts as 'education' is never questioned, but rather;

*Political culture* is seen as a relatively persistent set of common values . . . the problem arises when the 'common values' referred to are postulated and used as an explanation of the maintenance of a particular order. (however), values . . . can only be seen as constructed and legitimated by groups with common concern in particular historical contexts; these have to be explained not used as explanations. (Young, 1972, pp. 197—8)

Young argues that Manzer's definition of politics as the process by which social values are authoritatively allocated, presupposes the consensus on values that it is the aim of his (Young's) paper to treat as problematic.[6] Young speculates that beyond and underlying the apparent and superficial shared understandings of what counts as education lies conflict on values. The new sociology of education is to discover the values and meanings which underlie the manifest consensus on values by treating the shared understandings of what counts as education as problematic:

> sociological questions for research in education (or politics or industry for that matter) can only be posed by not accepting the ideas and institutions of the system that those involved in it are constrained to take as granted. This is true for . . . categories like teacher and pupil or even what counts as education, ability and achievement. (Young, 1972, p. 201)

Sociological questions, then, cannot be posed in terms of the ideas of the social actors involved but, according to Young, they can *only* be posed by taking them as a starting point, that is, as the basic data of sociological enquiry which is to discover underlying meanings. Why should sociological enquiry take this form? Why is this the only form that sociological enquiry in the new sociology of education can take? Young gives us his answer when he tells us that, in effect, the 'new' sociology is not new but is the 'social scientific' method of Alfred Schutz, for whom everyday experiences that are taken for granted are the basic data of social science. As we shall see, this form of sociological enquiry, to which Young's new directions for the sociology of education are pointing confines social science to an elaborate but nonetheless speculative realm.

## (ii)  THE 'PHENOMENOLOGICAL' SOCIOLOGY OF ALFRED SCHUTZ AND THE 'POLITICS' OF EDUCATIONAL KNOWLEDGE

In the argument that educational knowledge has an underlying political character, there is said to exist a certain stock of knowledge from which a stock of socially approved knowledge finds its way into the educational curriculum. It is this stock of socially approved knowledge which is taken for granted by educators and officials as what counts as educational knowledge. In the consciousness of educational 'actors' (i.e. teachers, officials, etc.) this stock of knowledge is said to be regarded as non-political. Young, however, is convinced as to the political nature of educational knowledge, which is expressed in the nature of its *control*. This control results in the 'imposition of meaning' and thus leads Young to questions about how and by whom meaning is given to education. His project is the discovery of the precise character of the 'approval process'. His method is to discover underlying political characteristics of what is taken for granted as educational knowledge by treating the latter as problematic.

This focuses on how priorities for 'curriculum development' are defined which would involve exploring the definitions of educational knowledge that are held by different groups. One can view these priorities as *constituted in the interaction* in particular settings, of *agents* of educational support (primarily those from business, local government and the Ministry, who are in a position to allocate resources), and of educational practice (teachers) . . . one might explore linkages between the financing, control and practice of education more generally . . . (Young, 1972, p. 196)

A considerable problem with Young's writings is that there is little more than speculation as to the 'political' character of educational knowledge. Young indicates, quite explicitly, that his papers are merely guidelines; suggested directions for the new sociology of education. Even his *On the Politics of Educational Knowledge*, which is the nearest he comes to a substantive account of the alleged mechanisms of the political character of educational knowledge, does little more than delineate some 'preliminary considerations' and 'raise questions', as he puts it.

However, Young is confident in the guidelines he is setting out. These guidelines for the new sociology of education point to a study of meanings and priorities in particular settings, such as the Schools Council. For it is here, and in other settings, that what is constituted in the interaction of agents may be studied in order to, reveal underlying political priorities. Fortunately for the new sociology the methods of this 'scientific research' have already been 'pointed to' in the work of Alfred Schutz. Young tells us that

Schutz treats the institutional definitions or typifications (whether of education or families or politics) as the intersubjective reality which men have constructed to give meaning to their world; therefore though they are part of the accepted world of everyday life for teachers, mothers and politicians, they can become the objects of sociological enquiry. In other words, if 'knowledge' or 'what is taken for knowledge' is ideal-typical in construction, Schutz is pointing to a study of the 'construction' of subjects, disciplines and syllabi as sets or provinces of meaning which form the basis of the intersubjective understandings of educators. The school curriculum becomes just one of the mechanisms through which knowledge is 'socially distributed'. (Young, 1971, p. 27)

Schutz himself makes a distinction within the notion of the 'social distribution of knowledge'. He argues that there is one aspect of the social distribution of knowledge which, to a certain extent, is the opposite of socially derived knowledge. He calls this socially approved knowledge:

Any knowledge . . . receives additional weight if it is accepted not only by ourselves but by other members of our in-group. I believe my own experiences to be correct beyond doubt if others whom I consider competent corroborate what I found . . . If I consider my father, my priest, my government to be authoritative, then their opinions have special weight and this weight itself has the character of imposed relevance. The power of socially approved knowledge is so extended that what the whole in-group approves—ways of thinking and acting, such as mores, folkways, habits—is simply taken for granted; it becomes an element of the relatively natural concept of the world, although the source of such knowledge remains entirely hidden in its anonymity. (Schutz, 1964, p. 133)

A major theoretical problem which arises here, in Schutz's formulations, also persists throughout Young's work. The problem, which as we shall see also arises in the formulations of Illich and of Freire, centres on how the authors conceive of the 'imposition of meanings' as taking place. For Schutz 'he who lives in the social world is a free being: his acts proceed from spontaneous activity' (Schutz, 1967, p. 227). How then is it possible for others to impose on the consciousness of an essentially free human subjectivity?[7] Schutz's suggestion, above, is that people bring it on themselves by choosing to consider various others as competent (in Schutz's example, father, priest, government, etc.). If, on the other hand, it is the decision as to who we recognize as competent that is imposed on us then we are returned to the original question, to which we have no answer in Schutz's formulations. As we shall see, Young's solution involves him in a similar theoretical incoherence in which he asserts that the human subject is essentially free in that it is capable of personal choice (for example in 'taking sides'), whilst also asserting the possibility of the 'imposition of meaning'. We shall examine Young's formulations in more detail in section B. For the moment we shall proceed with our examination of the Schutzian social science which Young would have us bring to the new sociology of education.

For Schutz, as for Young, the 'zone of things taken for granted' is the area from which all enquiry starts and which all enquiry presupposes. It reveals itself as the sediment of previous 'acts of experiencing'. For Schutz all knowledge is the product of acts of experiencing and, therefore, enquiry into knowledge involves enquiry into the structure of acts of experiencing, either of the past or the recent, which inhabits the consciousness, where it is taken for granted. The latter is the basic data of social science. The constructs used by the social scientist are said to be constructs of the second degree, namely, constructs of the constructs made by the actors on the social scene. The social scientist studies the construction of 'typified meanings'.

> Our knowledge in daily life is not without hypothesis, inductions, and predictions, but they all have the character of the approximate and the *typical*. The ideal of everyday knowledge is not certainty, nor even probability in the mathematical sense, but just likelihood ... . the consistency of this system of knowledge is not that of natural laws, but that of typical sequences and relations. This kind of knowledge and its organisation I should like to call 'cook-book knowledge'. (Schutz, 1964, p. 73)

For science, as for everyday life, 'cook-book knowledge' or the 'ideal-typical' represents its basic data according to Schutz's formulations, and

> What counts is the typical character of the occurrence within a typified situation. Thus, in this organization of the social world by the human being living naively in it, we already find the germ of the system of types and typical relations . . . the essential feature of *scientific method*. (Schutz, 1964, p. 71; emphasis added)

For social science, as for everyday life and for cookery, the proof of its method is in the eating. Schutz tells us how the social scientist should proceed, now that he has his recipe. It is this procedure, to which Schutz is pointing, which is the new direction for the sociology of education according to M. F. D. Young.

The social scientist observes certain facts and events within social reality, which refer to human activity, and he constructs typical behaviour or 'course-of-action' patterns from what he has observed. For the new sociology of education these typifications are the institutional definitions of knowledge or what is taken for knowledge, which are ideal-typical in construction and which are sets or provinces of meanings which form the basis of the intersubjective understandings of educators. The sociologist is able to investigate the structure of educational knowledge, following Schutz's directions, by treating knowledge as an ideal-typical construction which is susceptible to sociological enquiry because it is a socially constructed entity. These typifications are the data which the social scientist uses, and given certain conditions on the part of the scientist himself, they can do their work. How shall he proceed?

Everyone, to become a social scientist, must make up his mind to put somebody else instead of himself as the centre of this world, namely the observed person. . . . The first and fundamental consequence of this shift in the point of view is that the scientist replaces the human beings he observes as actors on the social stage by puppets created by himself and manipulated by himself. What I call 'puppets' correspond to the technical term 'ideal types' which Weber[8] has introduced into social science. (Schutz, 1964, p. 81)

Although for social science the basic data is the common-sense under-standings of everyday life, that is, the concepts formed by the social scientist are constructs formed in common-sense thinking by the actors on the social scene, the constructs of human interaction patterns formed by the social scientist are of an entirely different kind. Scientific knowledge is guaranteed because the social scientist considers his position within the social world, and the system of relevances attached thereto, as irrelevant to his scientific undertaking.

His stock of knowledge at hand is the corpus of his science . . . *scientifically ascertained* . . . to this corpus of science belong . . . the rules of procedure which *have stood the test*, namely, the methods of his science, including the methods of forming constructs in a scientifically sound way. This stock of knowledge is of quite another structure than that which man in everyday life has at hand. (Schutz, 1962, p. 39; emphasis added)

Scientificy is ascertained by the willingness of the social scientist who wishes to analyse the basic concepts of the social sciences 'to embark upon a laborious philosophical journey, for the meaning structures of the world can only be deduced from the most primitive characteristics of consciousness' (Schutz, 1967, p. 12). The conditions of scientific production of knowledge of social reality, then, are in the *attitudes* of the scientist, in his 'willingness to philosophise', and in the existence of an *ultimate* scientific method which has stood some unexplained and unexplainable test. Science is thus the product of scientific procedure which has 'stood the test' and is *guaranteed* by the social scientist adopting the scientific attitude. To the 'corpus of science' belong the scientific procedures and their test, and the social scientist *has to take it for granted*, according to Schutz. Scientific procedures *and* their test are, therefore, the *ultimate criteria* for science. As such they are not subject to scientific explanation, they are the *pre-conditions* of scientific explanation. It is this fundamentally dogmatic conception of science and social scientific method which Young insists should be the basis of the new sociology of education when he insists that the new directions have already been pointed to in the work of Alfred Schutz. How, then, shall our new sociologist in education proceed?

## (iii) THE NEW SOCIOLOGIST IN EDUCATION: PUPPET-MASTER AND CONJURER

Following Schutz, the new sociologist sets out to observe certain events as caused by human activity, and he begins to establish a *type* of such proceedings. He then co-ordinates with these typical acts, typical actors as their performers. One suggested 'setting' which the new sociologist might observe is, as we have already noted, the Schools Council,[9] where educational knowledge is the product of priorities as constituted in the interaction of agents of educational support.

With the ideal-typical constructs of what counts as educational knowledge as his basic data, the social scientist imputes a fictitious consciousness to these agents of educational support and of educational practice. Having endowed his 'puppets' with certain underlying characteristics the new sociologist in education attempts to fit the known, ideal-typifications (in this example, of what counts as educational knowledge) to the underlying characteristics with which the fictitious consciousness of his puppets have been endowed. In this way, it is alleged that it is possible to establish the relationship between (in this case), the political character of the underlying priorities of those who are said to approve educational curricula, and the more readily available shared understandings of what counts as knowledge. When a 'good' fit has been established between the outcome of the interacting fictitious consciousnesses imputed by the new sociologist, and the ideal-typical shared understandings of what counts as educational knowledge, the sociologist may 'read off' the appropriate underlying characteristics of the agents in interaction, and the political character of educational knowledge is revealed.

This elaborate procedure or puppetry should not, however, obscure from us that having started only with available meanings Young's new sociologist appears to emerge with otherwise unavailable meanings. The suggestion seems to be that we gain something for nothing. The puppet-master/sociologist is also a conjurer. However, this sleight of hand is revealed for what it is when we note that it was the sociologist/conjurer himself who imputed the very results which appear to emerge. In this case Young's new sociology *already* 'knows' that there are underlying political characteristics to the social approval process of what counts as educational knowledge. What now appear as conclusions were the initial imputations, the very beginnings of Young's project for the new sociology of education. In *Knowledge and Control* we are told that we can;

> begin to raise questions about relations between the power structure and curricula, the access to knowledge and the opportunities to legitimize it as 'superior', and the relation between knowledge and its function in different kinds of society. (Young, 1971, p. 36)

Moreover, the study of the Schools Council only 'reveals' what Young *already* 'knew' to be the function of knowledge in societies.

> The Schools Council, through its legitimation of curricula that might be characterised in Bourdieu's terms as based on class cultures, together with the schools, maintains the class structure of which they are a reflection. (Young, 1972, p. 210)

We can draw several conclusions here. Firstly, it is only an *a priori* understanding on the part of the social scientist which rescues the connection between the 'common-sense understandings' and the 'underlying character-istics' from the realm of the speculative. That is, the connection is *nothing but speculation*. This realm of speculation is masked by an explicit argument concerning the causal mechanism of class structure maintenance. This masking 'hides' the theoretical emptiness of the speculative, which is the 'theory' of that causal mechanism. In explicitly arguing that class structure is maintained by its own reflection at the cultural level, Young argues that the class structure secures its own conditions of existence. Class structure is thus conceived as a cause immanent in its effects, reproducing the conditions of its own existence. In the teleology of this 'structural causality',[10] the mechanism of reproduction is theorized at the speculative level of subjective meanings; that is, in the speculation on 'imposition of meanings' which represents the 'politics of educational knowledge' in Young's conception. Consequently, as we shall see below, any conception of social change which Young posits, must involve the theoretical elaboration of some *other* mechanism, which must then involve theoretical incoherence with respect to the conception of the politics of educational knowledge so far elaborated. As we shall see, this theoretical incoherence is itself masked by the insistence on the radical nature of the new sociology of education. It is to this 'radicalism' that we now turn our attention.

## B. RADICALISM AND EPISTEMOLOGY IN THE NEW SOCIOLOGY OF EDUCATION

Despite the severe theoretical limitations associated with its speculative character, the new sociology urges its followers towards its 'radicalism'. In his paper 'Taking Sides Against the Probable: Problems of Relativism and Commitment in Teaching and the Sociology of Knowledge', however, Young advises us of a number of concerns which he recognizes as arising from his conception of knowledge and of educational knowledge in particular. These concerns, he tells us, centre on the problem of relativism and the related problem of the undermining of the action of teachers.

> The first concern arises out of the increasing relevance for redefining our problems, that many of us working in the sociology of education, have found in what for the moment I shall refer to as 'The sociology of knowledge'. The enthusiasm with which I certainly have accepted this redefinition, has perhaps allowed the problem of relativism to be too readily dismissed (often as 'just the philosophers' problem'). The problem here is of cultural relativism, where if all knowledge is a social and historical product, then we have no grounds for deciding the worth, truth or value of anything—something both as teachers and as ordinary men and women we have to do all the time. That then is the first concern. The second concern is with teachers, who can read this relativism, and in fact much sociological enquiry in education [ . . . ] as not so much redefining problems, but 'undermining action'—their action as teachers. (Young, 1973b, p. 210)

The problem, as Young sees it then, is one in which his epistemological position has repercussions for the action of teachers who accept his arguments. For if, as Young's conception of knowledge argues, there cannot be any educational knowledge which does not involve imposing meanings which are of a political character, what then should the teacher who is 'committed' to something other than the imposing of meanings of a political character (to use Young's own phrases), teach? I have no argument against committed teachers. However, it is a consequence of Young's own argument that teachers cannot be committed both to teaching and at the same time to his educational philosophy/sociology.

For Young there are *given* differing subjective meanings whilst any teaching necessarily involves the imposition of other meanings, a form of action that is unacceptable to these teachers, who are nonetheless committed to something which the new sociology and sociological enquiry in general, undermines. It would seem that education (if education is at all possible) should be concerned only with the meanings, ideas, myths of particular groups who share these sets of meanings. Clearly, what these teachers might be committed to is *teaching*. That is, to teaching things which do not fall into the category of the shared meanings, in this case, of groups of children. Any such teaching is undermined by the new sociology of education because it is condemned as the imposition of meaning which is political in character. In short, education is political indoctrination, irrespective of its content, because the curriculum is the end result of a knowledge selection process which is dominated by certain political interests. Either, teaching is to be undermined or the new sociology of the politics of educational knowledge is to be abandoned.

In the course of his paper, 'Taking Sides . . .', and in a paper entitled 'Educational Theorizing: A Radical Alternative', Young attempts an escape from these problems by refusing to engage in serious debate in reply to his critics. Instead he launches an attack on his own caricature of what he variously calls 'theorizing', 'philosophy' and 'academic critiques' in general. His aim is to discredit all in favour of the subjectivism and relativism which characterize his notion of radicalism. In his caricature Young tells us that:

> the 'crutches' offered by 'objectivist' theories of knowledge may be seen as an attempt to evade something fundamental like being a person, historically and socially constructed, and as such, oneself responsible. (Young, 1973b, p. 213)

His 'escape' is further effected by then hiding behind an explicit 'radicalism' in which the enterprise of sociologists, philosophers and educational theorists, who are no longer avoiding human and personal commitments,

> is not the niggling of academic critiques, but the political commitment to engage with others; teachers, parents, students, pupils . . . [involving] a *radicalism* towards the possibilities of change . . . [for] If we start to ask what this kind of radicalism means in the contexts we find ourselves, we may also make 'educational theorizing' a way of learning to *change the world*. (Young, 1973a, p. 11; emphasis added)

Here, radicalism means a political commitment which involves a rejection of established educational theorizing in order to establish a new form of educational theorizing, and it means radicals recognizing the '*absolute* character of anyone's actions' (Young, 1973b, p. 220). For action, 'whether in research, teaching or whatever, is a decision, not a private decision, but a public or political one to 'insert ourselves in a course of events' (Young, 1973b, p. 219).

Young argues that in the 'versions of the "philosophical escape"', philosophers, sociologists and educational theorists avoid the immediacy of events by finding 'ways of avoiding specifically human and personal commitments' (ibid., p. 220), and in doing so they also fail to grasp a radical new idea of truth. For,

> philosophical claims, forms of knowledge or whatever are inevitably caught up in the culture they belong to . . . the question 'where does he speak from?' is one that has to be directed to both sociologists and philosophers alike . . . this is not a denial of the possibility of truth . . . but a *radical new idea of truth*. Our situation is not the source of error, but is that which gives meaning to what we know, what exists for us and is *the point of origin of all truth*. (Young, 1973a, p. 10; emphasis added)

Thus, Young at first argues that there *is* a problem of relativism but forgets the problem which is then offered as the solution. Young's 'problem of relativism' is never solved and indeed rather than attempting to defend the new sociology against the charge of relativism, he contends that all knowledge, in the radical new idea, is subjective and relative; and this radicalism informs us that 'the epistemological problems raised earlier are *fundamentally human* ones' (Young, 1973b, p. 220; emphasis added).

What characterizes the new sociology is its *radical sociologists* who are committed to grasping the immediacy of events. They are, Young tells us, like the French resistance fighters 'taking sides against the probable', that is, 'challenging much of our social life which is concerned with living with the probable, and much of our social science' which is 'concerned with discovering the probable' (ibid., p. 220). What makes the new sociology different from this old social science is its *radical sociologists*, who have a personal commitment, a 'commitment to human liberation'. This commitment which characterizes the radical, appears to solve all epistemological problems and informs and directs all actions, including political actions. Indeed, it is a political act in itself. In this circularity of 'politics' and 'commitment' we are told nothing about either, but this *empty circularity* is as far as Young's new sociology can take us, for, 'it is *in the end* personal commitments that are the grounds for action, whether that action is deciding what to do in the classroom or the 'adequacy' of a researcher's account (Young, 1973b, p. 221; emphasis added).

Unlike previous analysis of the politics of educational knowledge, which,

Young argued above, rested on unexplained sets of values, Young's own analysis rests on a notion of personal commitments. In Young's analysis politics is in the end (i.e. ultimately) a matter of personal commitment. The difference between the previous analysis of the politics of educational knowledge and the new sociology is that, in the former, Young tells us, values are unexplained (in *his* sociology they are *unexplainable* as we have seen), whilst in the latter it is personal commitments which are both unexplained and unexplainable. They are an *ultimate* realm in Young's conception of the new sociology of education.

If we follow Young's new directions for the sociology of education, with regard to the sociology of the politics of educational knowledge, we are lead from a puppet show to a conjuring act, in which sociology becomes nothing but speculation about underlying values, and on to a conception of politics based on personal commitments whose explanation is impossible in that they inhabit an ultimate realm. We are offered an extreme subjectivism and relativism, not even disguised but merely renamed 'radicalism', and a new sociology whose radical nature is characterized by a mysticism with regard to meanings, values, etc., which are its chosen realm. Young's conception of sociology is of a speculative project which is condemned to fail to achieve its stated aim of explanation of underlying values and which leads to a conception of politics which rests on a sphere of *ultimate personal commitment*.

We have seen that teaching is undermined by the new sociology of education because it is condemned as the imposition of meanings of a political character. For Young, education is political indoctrination, irrespective of its content, because the curriculum is the end result of a knowledge selection process which is dominated by certain political interests. We have not been concerned with an empirical refutation of Young's position, but rather, to show that the assessment of the political character of education is impossible within the 'phenomenological' perspective. With respect to the activity of teachers, we have argued that either teaching is to be undermined or the new sociology of education must be abandoned.

Rather than being abandoned the new sociology has been taken up with enthusiasm by a number of sociologists of education. One of the best known of Young's followers is Nell Keddie. By way of an illustration we shall examine Keddie's formulations in order to demonstrate that they lead to an explicit antagonism towards contemporary education. Whilst questioning certain assumptions in educational theorizing, her own arguments provide no means of effecting changes in the aspects of education of which she is critical.

In the introduction to *Tinker, Tailor . . . The Myth of Cultural Deprivation*, Keddie sets out to question teachers' alleged[11] 'taken for granted assumption' or 'myth' of cultural deprivation. For educational actors,

> ... the term becomes a euphemism for saying that working-class and ethnic groups have cultures which are at least dissonant with, if not inferior to, the 'mainstream' culture of the society at large. Culturally deprived children, then, come from homes where mainstream values do not prevail and are therefore less 'educable' than other children. The argument is that the school's function is to transmit the mainstream values of the society and the failure of children to acquire these values lies in their lack of educability. Thus their failure in school is located in the home, in the pre-school environment, and not within the nature and social organization of the school which 'processes' the children into achievement rates. (Keddie, 1973, p. 8)

Keddie argues that it is the *institutionalization* of the concept that 'has increasingly put these children at a disadvantage in terms of what is expected from them from the day they enter school', and when she declares that her concern is to 'raise problems about the appropriateness and consequences of the concept of cultural deprivation' it is not the *concept* of cultural deprivation that is to be investigated but the consequences of its institutionalization; the consequences of its alleged adoption by teachers as one of their assumptions. Keddie's critique is not directed at the concept of cultural deprivation but at *teachers* and teachers' culture. Keddie's arguments merely urge teachers to change their subjective viewpoint. Teachers are urged towards a reorientation in which they will come to regard the culture of 'working-class and ethnic groups' as no less valid than the 'mainstream culture' that they as teachers are alleged to represent. This might lead to

> ... a redirection of educational research away from attempting to formulate how to make children more like teachers. It would be more sensible to consider how to make teachers more bicultural, more like the children they teach, so that they can understand forms of English which they do not themselves use as native speakers. (ibid., p. 10)

In the 'taken for granted assumptions' of teachers it is the culture of the children which is said to be regarded as deficient. Keddie merely changes the articulation of cultures, and the 'mainstream culture' of the teachers is now categorized as deficient in that it does not encompass that of the child.

In this 'redefinition' of the 'problem' the educational circumstances of certain groups of children remain largely the same. It is still argued that some

. . . children come from poor homes, often slums, live in overcrowded conditions which deny access to privacy, and lack variety in their surroundings which leads to stimulus-deprivation. (ibid., p. 11)

Keddie's 'solution' to educational problems, that is, her redefinition of the problems,[12] finds the source of the educational underachievement, of children living in such conditions, in the deficiency of teachers' mainstream culture. Her explanation of underachievement relies on *cultural* explanation, insisting that its source is in the dissonance of the child's and the teacher's culture. Furthermore, the insistence on the primacy of the everyday experiences of children involves an antagonism towards contemporary educational practice, and this position is clearly advocated in Keddie's discussion of Neil Postman's paper, *The Politics of Reading*.[13]

In asking what reading is for, what literacy is about, Postman argues that school education as it is practised must be a form of social control with political implications (using both the narrower and wider meanings of power and coercion). This, together with his suggestions of how the mass media might become an integral, natural and meaningful part of school education, is the paper's strength. Not only is it clear that school education is historically and technologically stagnant but that the insistence on literacy is peculiar to school education and not to the life-worlds of learners (who would here include teachers) in most other contexts of their social lives. (Keddie, 1973, p. 16)

Keddie attempts to substantiate the radical critique of contemporary educational practice through a number of other illustrations. It is argued that the everyday experiences of children are valid in themselves in that everyday activity involves thinking and reasoning, which is at least as complex as that involved in mathematics, reading or writing. She argues that papers by Labov and Gladwin,[14]

suggest that so-called minority-group cultures may be seen as not only adequate in their own right, but perfectly competent to conceptualize logically and imaginatively. The perception of these cultures as deficient seems to arise from the ignorance of those who belong to what they perceive as the dominant cultural tradition. (ibid., p. 13)

Commenting on Gladwin's paper, which includes an account of the Trukese[15] activity of navigating a sailing canoe, Keddie insists that,

We have, after reading his paper, to ask not only whether navigating a boat is not like driving a car, but whether either is really qualitatively different from doing a sum or reading a book. (ibid., p. 17)

Keddie's enthusiasm for 'practical experience' obscures from her the particular utility of numeracy and literacy. It is *not* a question of whether navigating a boat is different from the skills of numeracy and literacy, but that the latter facilitates the capacity to learn not only to navigate but to engage in other activities. This is not to argue against practical experience but to argue that (in this example) whilst the child who can *only* navigate cannot, by definition, read and write, those who can read and write can *learn* not only to navigate but to engage in other activity—cultural *and* political.[16]

Keddie's romanticism[17] towards everyday experiences involves her in an explicit antagonism towards contemporary education and contemporary educational practice which is concerned with teaching children concepts and skills including those of literacy and numeracy. The consequences for educational practice of the implementation of her 'radical' pedagogy is the *deprivation* of children of their formal education. Anthropological radicalism is not, of course, confined to Keddie. See, for example, Sir Edmund Leach's article 'Literacy be damned', amongst others.[18]

## CONCLUSION

The major problem with the mish-mash which M. F. D. Young presents as the new directions for the sociology of education, and as the sociology of the politics of educational knowledge, is the lack of any rigorous theoretical argument. However, if we follow the references which are meant to guide the new sociology, we find that the 'new directions' are *mis*-directions. In directing the new sociology to the 'phenomenological' sociology of Alfred Schutz, Young's formulations lead to a sociology whose realm is speculation on meanings. The conception of knowledge which Young acquires from the so-called phenomenologists leads to an extreme relativism and subjectivism from which he attempts to escape by appealing to the radicalism of this very relativism and subjectivism. Unlike previous conceptions of the politics of educational knowledge, which he argues fails to explain subjective values, the new sociology posits a realm of *ultimate* personal commitment. Young's conception of radicalism which informs and directs political action and defines his conception of politics inhabits this realm and is therefore, in Young's conception, beyond the realm of investigation. It is not surprising then that his project in the sociology of the politics of educational knowledge collapses into speculation.

Young's conception of knowledge is combined with conceptions of politics and radicalism adopted from the work of Freire and Illich. In the following chapter we will examine the work of Freire and discuss its limitations, whilst Illich is examined in chapter 4. In the reference to Freire and to Illich, and in his own formulations, Young commits the new sociology of education to an object of enquiry which is a fundamentally idealist and teleological conception of man. Here, politics is the mere epiphenomenon of the process of the history of man, and it is an epiphenomenon whose characteristics inhabit a realm of ultimate personal commitment. The concept of radicalism which characterizes Young's concept of politics is totally indeterminate in that it is subsumed under this ultimate sphere of personal commitment.

It is clear that these *mis*-directions cannot lead to any theoretical advance for the sociology of education, and also that they cannot be the grounds for any rigorous educational policy formulation as our examination and discussion of Keddie has demonstrated. Finally, it should be pointed out that the theoretical objections raised in this chapter to 'phenomenological' sociology have consequences for a whole range of work under the heading of 'classroom observation.' This is particularly so for work which involves the imputation of meanings to behaviour (which includes most of such work) whether or not it refers to itself as phenomenological sociology.

# 3 Marxism, Ideology and Sociology of Education

It was argued in the Introduction that a distinction should be drawn between Marxist and radical theories of education, but it is not suggested here that such a distinction be made on the grounds that Marxism holds any privileged status. On the contrary, it has already been suggested not only that Marx and Engels and Lenin offer no systematic elaboration of a theory of education, but further, that there can be no general Marxist theory of education. This chapter examines the specific attempts to extend Marxist theory into contemporary theory of education, which appear in the work of Louis Althusser and Paulo Freire, and it discusses their limitations. In chapter 5 the work of Samuel Bowles and Herbert Gintis, who claim to be 'influenced by Marxism', will be examined. In particular the notion of the role of education in the reproduction of forces of production will be examined and criticized.

In discussing the problems which surround the proposals for a Marxist theory of education it will become clear that, the absence of such a theory in classical Marxism apart, many problems arise out of the attempt to utilize Marxist concepts themselves. That is to say, the attempt to utilize Marxist concepts in a construction of a Marxist theory of education introduces theoretical problems which are *internal* to Marxist discourse as such, as well as additional problems which construction itself might bring. Despite these problems the current infatuation of a number of sociologists and educational theorists with certain interpretations of Marxism has led to an influx of some of these interpretations into contemporary sociology of education. These different interpretations are to no small extent due to the ambiguous nature of Marxist theory itself. It is not suggested here that out of these ambiguities a 'correct' or 'true' Marxism can be teased and then used as a discourse against which other discourse (Marxist or non-Marxist) can be read in order to determine its 'correctness' or 'validity'. On the contrary, the mode of critique in this book involves an examination of the internal relations between the concepts within the discourse in question.

We will examine Althusser's attempt[1] to develop a general theory of ideology via a theory of institutions which includes what Althusser calls the educational Ideological State Apparatus (ISA) which he conceives as the dominant ISA in mature capitalist social formations (societies). Althusser conceives this theoretical work as an extension of the Marxist theory of the State. Nevertheless, some sociologists of education find Althusser's formulations, and indeed those of Bowles and Gintis, strikingly similar in certain respects to the formulations of Talcott Parsons' structural-functionalist sociology. Now irrespective of whether or not such an observation is justified, to argue that Marxist writers propose formulations similar to those of Parsons or, say, Durkheim, does not in itself constitute a critique. If there are indeed similarities between accounts in distinct theoretical discourses then all that can be deduced is that certain formulations are not exclusively Parsonian or Marxist or whatever. The comparison of discourses cannot establish the 'correctness' nor the 'incorrectness' of a distinct discursive account.[2]

## A. IDEOLOGY, THE STATE AND EDUCATION IN CLASSICAL MARXISM

We have said that there have been a number of attempts to utilize Marxist concepts or to establish a Marxist theory of education despite the fact that Marx and Engels themselves wrote hardly anything on education, and when they did it was in relation to the issue in the context of the 19th century. What then is the pertinence of Marxism for educational theory?

A major connection which has been made between Marxist theory and theory of education has been made via the elaboration of the Marxist theory of the State and the concept of 'ideology'. Louis Althusser proposes the addition to the Marxist theory of the state of the notion of Ideological State Apparatuses (ISAs) of which the educational ISA is dominant in mature capitalist social formations. For Althusser, the state secures existing relations of production through the action of the ISAs and the Repressive State Apparatus. We shall discuss these concepts in some detail in section B. For the moment it should be noted that Althusser's formulations of the theory of ideology go beyond formulations in classical Marxism. A brief comment on certain aspects of classical Marxism is necessary before we proceed to an examination of Althusser's theory of ideology.

Classical Marxism, in its simplest form in Marx and Engels' polemic *The Communist Manifesto*, conceives of societies in the following manner.

The modern bourgeois society that has sprouted from the ruins of feudal society has not done away with class antagonisms. It has but established new classes, new conditions of oppression, new forms of struggle in place of the old ones.

Our epoch, the epoch of the bourgeoisie, possesses, however, this distinctive feature: it has simplified the class antagonisms. Society as a whole is more and more splitting up into two great hostile camps, into two great classes directly facing each other: Bourgeoisie and Proletariat. (*Selected Works*, p. 36)

Now the proletariat and the bourgeoisie are not the classes of modern sociology nor are they categories of the Registrar-General's classification. Furthermore, their 'antagonism' is not reducible to the antagonism of conflict depicted in the work of the 'conflict theorists' of modern sociology and political science such as Dahrendorf and others.[3] Class antagonism, for Marx and Engels, has a non-subjective, economic character which exists whether or not there is *open* conflict and hostility. Class antagonism is inscribed in the distinctly different relations to the means of production that characterize the proletariat and the bourgeoisie. Indeed, it is these *relations of production* which define the proletariat and the bourgeoisie. The bourgeoisie are the owners of the means of production, the factory buildings, the machines, the raw materials used in production, and they are the legal owners of the product. The proletariat on the other hand owns no productive property and has nothing to sell but its labour power. The relation to the means of production of proletarian labourers is as follows:

These labourers, who must sell themselves piecemeal, are a commodity, like every other article of commerce, and are consequently exposed to all the vicissitudes of competition, to all the fluctuations of the market. (ibid., p. 41)

In the formulations in classical Marxism the State is an instrument of the ruling class. In Marx's *The Civil War in France*, for example, the State is a machine, a centralized power with organs or an apparatus of repression. Under capitalist relations of production the State is the instrument of the bourgeoisie, the ruling class. For Lenin, the ruling class 'wield(s) a certain apparatus of coercion, an apparatus of violence'. The apparatus may take on different appearances from time to time; 'armed contingencies of troops, prisons, and other means of subjugating the will of others by force' (Lenin, 1919).

Marxism opposes the conception of the State as a neutral force above, and arbitrating over, the conflicts of society and insists that it is a repressive and coercive force in the hands of, and intervening in the interests of, the ruling classes, the bourgeoisie and its allies, against the proletariat. In capitalist society it functions to secure for the ruling class the conditions which enable it to dominate and subject the working class to the process of appropriation of surplus value (capitalist exploitation).[4] The State is thus the class enemy of the workers and their families. It is in this context that the proposal for 'elementary education by the state' in the Programme of the German Workers' Party is castigated by Marx as 'altogether objectionable'. He adds that rather than 'appointing the state as the educator of the people! . . . the state has need, on the contrary, of a stern education by the people' (Marx, 1875, *Selected Works*, p. 333).

Marx is not, of course, opposed to public education but, rather, he contrasts this to the notion of 'education by the state'. The latter is quite different from

> Defining by a general law the expenditures on the elementary schools, the qualifications of the teaching staff, the branches of instruction, etc., and . . . supervising the fulfilment of these legal specifications by state inspectors. (ibid., p. 333)

Again, in *The Communist Manifesto* Marx and Engels argue for 'Free education for all children in public schools'. Clearly, Marx and Engels did not have in mind the 'public' schools of the private sector of British education, nor is their opposition to 'State education' an opposition to what today goes under the name of the State education system.[5] This point has to be stressed mainly for those radical sociologists of education who associate their opposition to contemporary education with Marxism. The objections already discussed apart, Marx's scepticism towards the demands for equal elementary education in the Programme of the German Workers' Party stem from his disbelief that 'in present-day society (*and it is only with this one has to deal*) education can be equal for all classes' (emphasis in the original). Marx was writing in 1875. The task of socialists today is to deal with *this* society, to seek out its limitations and possibilities.

The concept of ideology and the concept of the mechanisms of ideology in classical Marxism are far from unproblematic. At the centre of the theoretical problem is the ambiguity over the significance of the category of the individual human subject. In his Preface to the First German Edition of *Capital*, Marx insists that relations of production are not reducible to relations between individual human subjects.

> To prevent possible misunderstanding, a word. I paint the capitalist and the landlord in no sense *couleur de rose*. But here individuals are dealt with

only in so far as they are the personifications of economic categories, embodiments of particular class-relations and class-interests. My standpoint, from which the evolution of the economic formation of society is viewed as a process of natural history, can less than any other make the individual responsible for relations whose creature he socially remains, however much he may subjectively raise himself above them.

Thus it would appear that Marx is not concerned with human individuals except in terms of the economic categories, interests and relations they personify. Interests, or ideologies, are the ideologies not of individuals but of the classes or economic categories they personify. Nevertheless, in the 1859 Preface to *A Contribution to the Critique of Political Economy* Marx *is* concerned with the human form of economic agent. Designating the relations between the concepts of ideology and consciousness in the concepts of social formation and mode of production, relations of production are defined not in terms of the economic categories of proletariat and bourgeoisie, but in terms of relations in the process of production *between men*. For Marx here:

In the social production of their life, men enter into definite relations that are indispensable and independent of their will, relations of production which correspond to a definite stage of development of their material productive forces. The sum total of these relations of production constitutes the economic structure of society, the real foundation, on which rises a legal and political superstructure and to which correspond definite forms of social consciousness. The mode of production of material life conditions the social, political and intellectual life process in general. It is not the consciousness of men that determines their being, but, on the contrary, their social being that determines their consciousness. At a certain stage of their development, the material productive forces of society come in conflict with the existing relations of production, or— what is but a legal expression for the same thing—with the property relations within which they have been at work hitherto. From forms of development of the productive forces these relations turn into their fetters. Then begins an epoch of social revolutions. With the change of the economic foundation the entire immense superstructure is more or less rapidly transformed. In considering such transformations a distinction should always be made between the material transformation of the economic conditions of production, which can be determined with the precision of natural science, and the legal, political, religious, aesthetic or philosophic—in short, ideological forms in which men become conscious

of this conflict and fight it out. Just as our opinion of an individual is not
based on what he thinks of himself, so can we not judge of such a period of
transformation by its own consciousness; on the contrary, this consciousness must be explained rather from the contradictions of material life,
from the existing conflict between the social productive forces and the
relations of production. (Marx, 1859, *Selected Works*, pp. 182–3)

In these formulations an ideological level is conceived as an array of forms
which the consciousness inhabits. It is within these ideological forms, legal,
political, religious, aesthetic or philosophic, that men fight out the
contradictions of material life. Contradictions at the economic level, in the
material conditions of life in the mode of production, are fought out at a
level of consciousness which inhabits specific ideological forms. So in
classical Marxism ideology is conceived as a *form* of consciousness. Thus
despite their differences in conception of 'society' both sociological and
Marxist theories conceive the notion of ideology in a similar manner.
Ideology is conceived in terms of its *effects* in the consciousness of human
subjects. In Durkheimian sociology, of course, a collective consciousness
exists outside the world of conscious subjects. The reflection of the collective
consciousness in the individual consciousness of human subjects who
constitute the social whole, reflects the social solidarity of that whole. For
Durkheim, social solidarity is always already secured as an effect of an
external consciousness, the collective consciousness. In classical Marxism, or
at least at certain points in classical Marxism, ideology is also conceived in
terms of its effects in the consciousness of human subjects, but its source is not
conceived as existing outside the world of conscious subjects, but in the 'life
process' of men themselves. Definite forms of social consciousness are said to
correspond to the sum total of relations of production, and the mode of
production of material life conditions the social, political and intellectual life
process in general. Thus it is 'not the consciousness of men that determines
their being, but on the contrary, their social being that determines their
consciousness'. This formulation, which also appears in *The German
Ideology*, constitutes part of Marx and Engels' critique of a *specific* mode of
thought, namely the idealist thought of classical German Philosophy, and in
particular they are concerned to combat the political consequences of Left
Hegelianism and Feuerbachism. In *The German Ideology* Marx and Engels
draw up little more than a sketch of a concept of ideology in terms of
'consciousness' because they are more concerned with a specific ideology
rather than with a general theory of ideology. Nevertheless, they do
conceive ideology in terms of a socially conditioned form of false
consciousness of the real. This is also the case in parts of *Capital*.

In *Capital*, whilst he is concerned with a specific ideology or mode of thought (that of capitalists and their agents, and its consequences in their economic calculation) rather than with the elaboration of a general theory of ideology as such, Marx nevertheless reduces specific ideology to the product of a general theory. The finance capitalist, for example, sees the world differently from the wage slave. The capitalist's ideology/illusion is a function of his relations to reality itself. The places in the structure, the place of the capitalist, the place of the wage slave, that are the creation of specific social relations generate the ideologies that follow from them through the mechanism of experience (Hirst, 1976a).

Thus, on the one hand ideology/consciousness is economically determined—ideology is the necessary ideology of classes and their relations to the means of production—a general theory; on the other, ideology/consciousness is the specific misrecognition of the real. This process of misrecognition requires the concept of the individual human subject with the capacities to 'experience'. Thus, Marx's arguments on the specific ideology of individual capitalists involves on the one hand a sociologism and on the other a general theory of the subject, of the attributes necessary for it to function as an experiencing subject. Ideology is the false consciousness of the experiencing individual human subject:

> . . . it is self-evident that conceptions which arise about the laws of production in the minds of agents of capitalist production and circulation will diverge drastically from (these) real laws and will merely be the conscious expression of visible movements. The conceptions of the merchants, stockbroker, and banker are necessarily distorted. (Marx, *Capital*, Vol. III, p. 313)

On the one hand consciousness is the product of misrecognizing experience, on the other it is the mere expression of relations of production. The individual human subject is both necessary and unnecessary to the mechanisms of the production of ideology. In either conception Marx's notion of ideology involves him in an epistemological critique of ideology/consciousness because the 'real' is *his* theoretical discourse. Ideology is that which fails to correspond to the real; to Marx's discourse on capitalism and capitalist relations of production. Ideology is false consciousness only by comparison to Marx's 'science'. For Althusser, ideology is not the distorted representation of the real. It therefore makes no sense whatever to say that Althusser's theory of ideology is not Marxist; it goes beyond Marx.

## B.  ALTHUSSER'S THEORY OF IDEOLOGY

Althusser argues that 'it is indispensable to *add* something to the classical definition of the State as a State apparatus' (1971, p. 134). However, Althusser's theory of ideology involves something more than the addition of the concept of the ISAs to the classical Marxist conception of the State. It involves a reconceptualization of the notion of ideology as such. Althusser attempts to develop a general theory of ideology and to elaborate the mechanisms of ideology. He argues that 'ideology interpellates individuals as subjects'. Let us begin with the conception of the ISAs.

We have already seen that classical Marxism conceives the State as an apparatus of repression, of coercion etc. Althusser proposes to retain this conception. He designates this aspect of the State the Repressive State Apparatus (RSA). In addition to the RSA Althusser proposes that there exists a number of Ideological State Apparatuses and he lists them as follows: the religious ISA (the system of the different Churches), the educational ISA (the system of the different public and private schools), the family ISA, the legal ISA, the political ISA (the political system, including the different Parties), the trade-union ISA, the communications ISA (press, radio and television etc.), and the cultural ISA (Literature, the Arts, sports etc.).

There are a number of distinctions between the RSA and the ISAs. Firstly there is *one* RSA whilst there is a plurality of ISAs. Secondly, and this seems to be the only reason why the RSA is conceived as a unity, the RSA belongs entirely to the public domain whereas the ISAs belong in part to the private domain. That is to say, Churches, political parties, trade-unions, families, some schools, most newspapers, cultural ventures etc. are private. Althusser anticipates the question as to why these private institutions should be regarded as part of *the State*. He argues that the very distinction between public and private is predicated on the State since the distinction is a distinction in bourgeois State law. However, Althusser goes on to argue that in any case the distinction between public and private is unimportant since 'private' institutions 'can perfectly well "function" as Ideological State Apparatuses' (p. 138). It has little consequence for his theory of ideology, but it might be noted in passing that the notion of the plurality of the ISAs as against the unity of the RSA as a distinguishing feature is effectively destroyed by the insistence on the non-distinction between the public and the private domain. This is because the unity of the RSA was based on the notion of it as an entirely *public* domain.[6]

The main distinction between the RSA and the ISAs is in the way that they function. It is not simply that the RSA functions by violence whilst the ISAs function by ideology. Rather, the RSA 'functions massively and predominantly *by repression* (including physical repression), while function-ing secondarily by ideology' (p. 138). The ISAs 'function massively and predominantly *by ideology*, but they also function secondarily by repression, even if ultimately, but only ultimately, this is very attenuated and concealed, even symbolic' (p. 138). Althusser illustrates this last point, arguing that,

> Thus the Schools and Churches use suitable methods of punishment, expulsion, selection, etc., to 'discipline' not only their shepherds, but also their flocks. The same is true of the Family . . . The same is true of the cultural IS Apparatus (censorship, among other things), etc. (p. 138)

(i)  THE MECHANISM OF IDEOLOGY IN ALTHUSSER'S THEORY

Althusser proposes a general theory of ideology. There are four theses: ideology is not false consciousness but rather ideology represents the imaginary relationship of individuals to their real conditions of existence; ideology has no history; ideology has a material existence; and ideology is speculary (it has the properties of a mirror) or rather, it is *doubly* speculary.
  Althusser argues that,

> We commonly call religious ideology, ethical ideology, legal ideology, political ideology, etc., so many 'world outlooks'. Of course, assuming that we do not live one of these ideologies as the truth (e.g. 'believe' in God, Duty, Justice, etc. . . .), we admit that the ideology we are discussing from a critical point of view, examining it as the ethnologist examines the myths of a 'primitive society', that these 'world outlooks' are largely imaginary, i.e. do not 'correspond to reality'. (p. 153)

Althusser argues that we nevertheless admit that ideologies make an allusion to reality, and that 'they need only be "interpreted" to discover the reality of the world behind their imaginary representation of that world (ideology = illusion/allusion)'. We can arrive at the conclusion that in ideology 'men represent their real conditions of existence to themselves in an imaginary form'. This position, however, leaves the problem of the question of why. Althusser rejects the 'solution' that men are simply duped, as well as the Marxist notion, in *The German Ideology*, that the cause is 'the material alienation which reigns in the conditions of existence of men themselves' because these interpretations take literally the thesis they presuppose and on which they depend. This thesis is that 'what is reflected in the imaginary representation of the world in an ideology is the conditions of existence of men, i.e. their real world' (p. 154).

In contradiction to this thesis Althusser proposes his thesis that it is not the real conditions of existence, their real world, that men represent to themselves in ideology, but 'it is *their relation* to these conditions of existence which is represented to them there' (p. 154; emphasis added). He argues that it is this relation which is at 'the centre of every ideological, i.e. imaginary, representation of the real world'. For Althusser ideology is not false consciousness; it is not a distorted representation of the real. On the contrary ideology is a representation of men's 'lived relation' to their conditions of existence and this lived relation is an imaginary relation. Althusser in effect rejects the sociologistic conception of ideology as the consciousness of the experiencing human subject which Marx and others expound.

It is important not to confuse the concept of the imaginary with the notion of 'imagination'. In order to elaborate the concept of the imaginary relation it is necessary to discuss the thesis that ideology is speculary. To do this we need to make something of a detour via the concept of the subject in epistemology in classical philosophy.

Althusser proposes the theses that ideology has a material existence, and ideology has no history. In the first of these two theses ideology has a material existence but not the 'same modality as the material existence of a paving-stone or a rifle' (p. 156). Nevertheless, ideology does not take the form only of ideas; it also takes the form of rituals and practices. They exist in particular in social institutions or ISAs. For example, sexism is not simply a set of ideas or an 'outlook' but consists also of definite rituals and practices; the practice of exclusion, for example, from certain aspects of social or economic life. The drawing of differential boundaries to numbers of new recruits to professional training in say law or medicine along sexual lines in certain countries is a good example of Althusser's notion of ideology as material practice with material effect.

On the other hand the notion that ideology has no history cannot be illustrated because this notion does not refer to specific ideologies. Indeed, Althusser readily admits that specific ideologies have histories. For Althusser, proposing a *general theory* of ideology, it is ideology *in general* that has no history, i.e. ideology is eternal 'in Freud's sense of the unconscious as eternal'. It is 'eternal' only on condition that 'there is no ideology except by the subject and for subjects'. By this Althusser means that,

> there is no ideology except for concrete subjects, and this destination for ideology is only made possible by the subject: meaning, *by the category of the subject* and its functioning. (p. 160)

Ideology 'interpellates or hails concrete individuals as concrete subjects'. We must discuss that concept of the subject.

In epistemology in classical philosophy individual human subjects live in, and in some epistemologies experience, the world of objects. A field of subject/object relations is supposed and a good deal of classical philosophy is concerned with the supposed relations between the knowing subject and the objects of the world which are the objects of his cognition. A number of philosophical positions are possible within the concept of a subject/object relation. The philosophical position which rejects the notion of the object or objective world and argues that nothing exists but thinking beings, minds and their ideas is called subjective idealism and is associated with Bishop George Berkeley.[7] In subjective idealism the surrounding world has no existence external to and independent of mind. On the other hand, the philosophical position which holds that the question as to whether or not there is an objective reality is an insoluble question is referred to as philosophical agnosticism and is associated with David Hume.[8] Hume held that there can be no basis for assuming an external cause to subjective perceptions and that the human consciousness is nothing but a stream of sensations. For Hume, science is simply the description of these sensations and is impotent to attain any scientific laws. In opposition to the subjective idealism of Berkeley and Hume's agnosticism, Bacon, Hobbes, Locke and the early French materialists considered independently existing objects, or matter, to be the source of sense experience. In empiricist epistemology knowledge of the objective world is said to be gained by the human subject by means of the process of abstraction.

In his critique of the empiricist concept of knowledge Althusser argues that in this conception 'to know is to abstract from the real object its essence, the possession of which by the subject is then called knowledge' (Althusser and Balibar, 1970, pp. 35–6). It is not necessary to go into Althusser's critique in detail here.[9] Nevertheless, it will be noticed that in all of the above conceptions the 'subject' is the centre of the knowledge process. That is to say, knowledge is *in* and *for* the subject; there is no knowledge without the subject and knowledge is only made possible by the subject. Althusser proposes to displace this centrality of the subject as a precondition to the production of scientific knowledge. This brings Althusser to a distinction between 'science' and 'ideology'; a distinction which he is not able to theoretically maintain within his system. However, what is important to note here is that *empiricism* which cannot produce scientific knowledge cannot produce ideological knowledge because it is not a process of knowledge production at all. Althusser argues that empiricism is an *impossible* epistemology. The formulation 'empiricist therefore ideological' cannot be maintained, and if ideology cannot simply be empiricism because empiricist epistemology is impossible, what when *is ideology* which interpellates individuals as subjects? Does Althusser not retain the subject of epistemology in classical philosophy?

To put the question another way; how, in rejecting the classical philosophical conception of the constitutive subject as the centre of the knowledge process and in rejecting the concept of empiricism as ideology because empiricism is an impossible epistemology, can Athusser still retain the concept of the subject in his concept of the process of ideology?

The subject is retained, not as an abstractive agent constitutive of the knowledge process but as an entity *a priori*.

> That an individual is always-already a subject, even before he is born, is nevertheless the plain reality, accessible to everyone and not a paradox at all. Freud shows that individuals are always 'abstract' with respect to the subjects they always-already are, simply by noting the ideological ritual that surrounds the expectation of a 'birth', that 'happy event' . . . Before its birth, the child is therefore always-already a subject. . . . (Althusser, 1971, pp. 164—5)

Althusser retains the concept of the subject because the concept of the imaginary relation presupposes a subject that 'lives' that relation. What happens, then, to subjects in the ISAs? The answer to this question takes the form of what Althusser calls his 'central thesis' that: 'all ideology hails or interpellates concrete individuals as concrete subjects' (p. 162). And again, 'the existence of ideology and the hailing or interpellation of individuals as subjects *are one and the same thing*' (p. 163) for 'there is no ideology except by the subject and for subjects' (p. 160).

A number of issues can now be raised. If subjects are always-already subjects then the interpellation of them as subjects cannot be the origin of ideology. We have already seen that ideology has no history; the breadth of the ISAs and the RSA suggests that ideology is so universal as to have no boundaries. We now find that ideology has no origin, indeed 'man is an ideological animal *by nature*' (p. 160). It might seem that material (to adopt Althusser's phrase) mechanisms are superfluous. Why the rituals and practices and the materiality of ideology in the ISAs and the RSA? Surely this speculative philosophical conception of 'Man' appears in lieu of, that is, it actually constitutes the major element of what Althusser designates to be accomplished by the process of the mechanisms of ideology. Nevertheless, Althusser proposes mechanisms of ideology in the concept of 'interpellation'. But does this concept not require that capacities of recognition be attributed to the subject? Are these attributes not the attributes ascribed in the speculative philosophical concept of man; the concept of his 'nature'? Indeed they are; it is this speculative philosophical anthropology which crowds the child's cradle with the tools of recognition. Subjects are, for Althusser, knowing subjects capable of recognition. It is here that Lacan's conception of the 'mirror-phase' is invoked.[10]

Althusser poses the thesis that ideology is 'speculary'. That is, it has the structure of a mirror but it is *doubly* speculary. In this thesis Althusser borrows from Jacques Lacan the concept of the mirror-phase which, for the latter, sheds light 'on the formation of the I as we experience it in psychoanalysis'.

> The human offspring, at an age when he is for a time, however short, outdone by the chimpanzee in instrumental intelligence, can nevertheless already recognise as such his own image in a mirror. This recognition manifests itself in the illuminatory mimicry of the *Aha-Erlebnis*, which Köhler sees as the expression of situational apperception, an essential moment of the act of intelligence. (Lacan, 1968, p. 71–2)

The mirror-phase is to be understood *as an identification*, that is to say, 'the transformation which takes place in the subject when he assumes an image'. Althusser utilizes Lacan's concept of the mirror-phase together with the Christian religious form of ideology to develop and illustrate his concept of ideology as doubly speculary as follows:

> We observe that the structure of all ideology, interpellating individuals as subjects in the name of a Unique and Absolute Subject is *speculary*, i.e. a mirror-structure, and *doubly* speculary: this mirror duplication is constitutive of ideology and ensures its functioning. Which means that all ideology is *centred*, that the Absolute Subject occupies the unique place of the Centre, and interpellates around it the infinity of individuals into subjects in a double mirror-connexion such that it *subjects* the subjects to the Subject, while giving them in the Subject in which each subject can contemplate its own image (present and future) the *guarantee* that this really concerns them and Him, and that since everything takes place in the Family (the Holy Family: the Family is in essence Holy), 'God will *recognise* his own in it', i.e. those who have recognised God, and have recognised themselves in Him, will be saved. (Althusser, 1971, p. 168)

In this analogy 'the dogma of the Trinity is precisely the theory of the duplication of the Subject (the Father) into a subject (the Son) and of their mirror-connexion (the Holy Spirit)'. The result is that 'caught in this quadruple system of interpellation as subjects, of subjection to the Subject, of universal recognition and of absolute guarantee, the subjects "work", they "work by themselves"'.

Its brilliance apart, what we can see here is the return of the concept of the subject. The subject is equivalent to the constitutive subject of classical philosophy with the exception that the process of ideological knowledge is conceived as a process in which the subject has a *self* constituting relation not to the object but to the Absolute Subject as object. But the 'possibility' of this process as a process of ideological knowledge is based on the necessity of the attribution to the concept of the subject of the tools required for recognition *a priori*. We are faced with the 'necessity' of a speculative anthropology or the alternative of having no coherent theoretical mechanism of ideology. Indeed such a mechanism is not necessary, for man is naturally ideological. Althusser's speculative anthropology presupposes not only the tools of recognition in subjects, it also presupposes their very nature.

## (ii)  THE REPRODUCTION OF THE FORCES OF PRODUCTION

In his paper 'Ideology and Ideological State Apparatuses' Althusser argues that 'the point of view of production' or that of productive practice is so integrated into our everyday consciousness that it is very difficult to think beyond it and to take the 'point of view of reproduction'. Nevertheless, it is this position, which Althusser claims to derive from Marx's *Capital*, that he 'takes' in his paper. To summarize, Althusser argues that in order to exist every social formation (society) 'must reproduce the conditions of production at the same time as it produces, and in order to be able to produce' (1971, p. 124). From the point of view of reproduction, then, it is essential that the forces of production and the existing relations of production are reproduced. For our purposes, here, we are concerned with the functions of the educational Ideological State Apparatus in securing certain aspects of reproduction, or more accurately, the functions which Althusser attributes to the educational ISA.

We have already noted that the educational ISA is ascribed the role of the dominant ISA. Althusser distinguishes between the reproduction of the relations of production and the reproduction of the productive forces. Let us first examine the functions ascribed to the educational ISA in the reproduction of the productive forces.

The productive forces consist of the means of production, i.e. the material conditions of production, raw material, fixed installations (buildings), instruments of production (machines), etc., and labour power. The reproduction of labour power takes place in the ISAs, and in particular in the family and the educational ISA. They are the site of the material reproduction of labour power but also the site of the reproduction of 'skills' and 'competence' and the reproduction of the subjection of labour power to the ruling ideology. The requirements of skill diversity of the socio-technical division of labour are achieved 'outside production: by the capitalist education system, and by other instances and institutions' (p. 127).

Althusser asks the question, 'What do children learn at school?' His answer is that they learn to read, to write, to add, that is, they learn a number of techniques and they also learn elements of scientific and literary culture. In short, they learn 'know-how'. However,

> besides these techniques and knowledges, and in learning them, children at school also learn the 'rules' of good behaviour, i.e. the attitude that should be observed by every agent in the division of labour, according to the job he is 'destined' for: rules of morality, civic and professional conscience, which actually means rules of respect for the socio-technical division of labour and ultimately the rules of the order established by class domination. (p. 127)

In other words, Althusser argues that the reproduction of labour power requires not only the reproduction of its skills but also the reproduction of its submission to the rules of the established order.

Now at this point it must be noted that Althusser has 'not yet approached the question of the *reproduction of the relations of production*' (p. 128). So far, he has been concerned only with the reproduction of the forces of production (which includes, as we have seen, the reproduction of labour power), and he insists on a distinction between the reproduction of the forces of production and the reproduction of the relations of production. After a long detour we arrive at the 'central question' which is: 'how is the reproduction of the relations of production secured?' (p. 141).

## (iii)  THE REPRODUCTION OF THE RELATIONS OF PRODUCTION

After elaborating his reasons for thinking that the School–Family couple has replaced the Church–Family couple, and that the educational ISA has displaced the religious ISA as the dominant ideological State apparatus in mature capitalist social formations, Althusser sets about delineating its functions and its mode of reproduction of the relations of production. Schools take

children from every class at infant-school age, and then for years, the years
in which the child is most 'vulnerable', squeezed between the family State
apparatus and the educational State apparatus, it drums into them,
whether it uses new or old methods, a certain amount of 'know-how'
wrapped in the ruling ideology (French, arithmetic, natural history, the
sciences, literature) or simply the ruling ideology in its pure state (ethics,
civic instruction, philosophy). (p. 147)

The individuals it has thus trained are 'ejected into production' by the
educational ISA after differing lengths of training; at the age of sixteen a
'huge mass of children' who are the workers and small peasantry. At a latter
age the educational ISA releases a batch which 'fills the posts of small and
middle technicians, white-collar workers, small and middle executives,
petty bourgeois of all kinds' and still later it releases a portion who are either
to 'fall into intellectual semi-employment, or to provide, as well as the
"intellectuals of the collective labourer", the agents of exploitation
(capitalists, managers), the agents of repression (soldiers, policemen, politicians, administrators, etc.) and the professional ideologists (priests of all
sorts, most of whom are convinced "laymen")' (p. 147).

Each mass ejected *en route* is practically provided with the ideology which
suits the role it has to fulfil in class society: the role of the exploited (with a
'highly-developed' 'professional', 'ethical', 'civic', 'national' and a-
political consciousness); the role of the agent of exploitation (ability to
give orders and enforce obedience 'without discussion', or ability to
manipulate the demagogy of a political leader's rhetoric), or of the
professional ideologist (ability to treat consciousness with respect, i.e. with
the contempt, blackmail, and demagogy they deserve . . . ) (p. 147)

At this stage the reader might be curious as to the similarity between these
functions and effects which are the means of securing the reproduction of the
relations of production, with the functions and effects which secure the
reproduction of labour power. In the latter, in addition to their material
reproduction, what was necessary was the securing in them of 'know-how',
attitudes, rules and respect for the socio-technical division of labour.
Althusser now maintains that,

it is by this apprenticeship in a variety of know-how wrapped up in the
massive inculcation of the ideology of the ruling class that the *relations of
production* in a capitalist social formation, i.e. the relations of exploited to
exploiters and exploiters to exploited, are largely reproduced. (p. 148)

Althusser's failure to maintain the distinction which he earlier insisted upon occurs because he now equates the relations of production with distribution of agents to places in the social division of labour. The relations of production are conceived as relations between individual human agents. The reproduction of the relations of production is nothing but the reproduction of labour power 'in ideology'.

To summarize, Althusser equates economic agents with human subjects and equates the relations of production with the functions assigned to economic agents in the social division of labour. An immediate problem, here, is that not all economic agents are human agents and capitalist relations of production need not involve *capitalists* in the form of human subjects. Non-human forms of agents may appear in the form of joint-stock companies or religious orders, for example. Furthermore, the concept of relations of production in Marxism includes not only relations between agents (human and non-human) but the *forms of relation* between agents. As Paul Hirst points out in his paper, 'Althusser and the Theory of Ideology', forms of circulation and exchange are examples of forms which

> have an objective existence and are not reproduced spontaneously by behaviours of the agents. Marx does not conceive the forms of circulation process in capitalism merely as a series of inter-relations between subjects, as exchanges generated through the correspondence of motivations of subjects. Marx . . . did not conceive exchange as inter-subjectivity. Thus to reproduce the agents is not to reproduce the forms of relations between them. (Hirst, 1976b, pp. 390–91)[11]

Our examination of the mechanism and functions of ideology in Althusser's theory brings us to the wider issues of social change (or transition) and reproduction. Althusser is concerned with the issue of the transition from capitalist relations of production to socialist relations of production. However, if relations of production are indeed secured via the State apparatuses how could the possibility of transition be conceived? In this theoretical problem we are returned to the problems inherent in the Marxist notions of 'base' and 'superstructure', already briefly introduced in section A of this chapter, and in particular the theoretical problem of the relations between them.

In his ISA paper Althusser argues that the 'greatest disadvantage of this representation of the structure of every society by the spatial metaphor of an edifice' (i.e. a structure with a base and a superstructure), 'is obviously the fact that it is metaphorical: i.e. it remains *descriptive*' (1971, p. 130). It is in going beyond the metaphor that Althusser elaborates the concept of the ISAs which we have just discussed, and specifically his concept of the superstructure and its alleged role in the reproduction of relations of production. The educational ISA, together with the other ISAs are conceived as parts of the structure which secure the reproduction of relations of production. This brings us to Althusser's concept of 'structural causality', and to the question posed above, i.e. if relations of production are indeed secured via the State apparatuses how can transition be conceived? For the concept of structural causality we must turn to *Reading Capital*.

## (iv) ALTHUSSER'S FUNCTIONALISM AND THE CONCEPT OF 'STRUCTURAL CAUSALITY'

Althusser's formulation of the problem of the reproduction of relations of production in capitalist social formations is beset with further problems. For example, he is concerned with the issue of the transition from capitalist relations of production to socialist relations of production. However, if relations of production are indeed secured via the State apparatuses how can such transition be conceived? In the book, *Reading Capital*[12] Althusser and Balibar propose the concepts of a transitional and a non-transitional mode of production.[13] Their concept of a non-transitional mode of production and their concept of the reproduction of that non-transitional mode of production cannot be consistent with an explicit claim to a possibility of transition. If the non-transitional mode of production is indeed non-transitional and always reproduces its own conditions of existence as effects, then how is the movement to a transitional mode of production to be conceived?

If transition is to be conceived as a possibility, then at stake here is the status of the concept of reproduction in the work of Althusser and Balibar. In the paper 'Marx's Immense Theoretical Revolution' (pp. 182–93), Althusser rejects the 'empiricist problematic' of Political Economy which thought of

the economic phenomena as deriving from a planar space governed by a transitive mechanical causality, such that a determinate effect could be related to an object-cause, a different phenomena; such that the necessity of its immanence could be grasped completely in the sequence of a given. (p. 182).

As a consequence of this rejection of linear causality, Althusser suggests that, if the field of economic phenomena is no longer this planar space but a deep and complex one, if economic phenomena are determined by their *complexity* (i.e., their structure), the concept of linear causality can no longer be applied to them as it has been hitherto. A different concept is required in order to account for the new form of causality required by the new definition of the object of Political Economy, by its 'complexity', i.e., by its peculiar determination: *the determination by a structure*. (p. 184).

It should be noted here, that for the authors of *Reading Capital* the radical break with the empiricist problematic of Political Economy, i.e., 'the new terrain which Marx opens up', Historical Materialism, does not entail a break with causality as such. It merely demands, according to Althusser and Balibar, a *new form* of causality. Thus, Althusser is led to pose the question,

> *by means of what concept or what set of concepts is it possible to think the determination of a subordinate structure by a dominant structure; In other words, how is it possible to define the concept of a structural causality?* (p. 186; emphasis in original)

Althusser suggests that classical philosophy has only two systems of concepts with which to think causality. Firstly, the Cartesian, which reduced causality to a transitive and analytical effectivity which 'could not be made to think the effectivity of a whole on its element, except at the cost of extraordinary distortions' (p. 186). Secondly, the Leibnizian concept of expression which deals with the effectivity of a whole on its elements. Althusser writes that,

> This is the model that dominates all Hegel's thought. But it presupposes in principle that the whole in question be reducible to an *inner essence*, of which the elements of the whole are then no more than the phenomenal forms of expression, the inner principle of the essence being present at each point in the whole, such that at each moment it is possible to write the immediately adequate equation: *such and such an element* (economic, political, legal, literary, religious, etc. in Hegel) = *the inner essence of the whole*. (pp. 186–7; emphasis in original)

Thus, the Hegelian category for the effectivity of the whole on its elements is conditional on not being a structure but a type of unity of a spiritual whole; a whole 'bathed' in the essence of its spiritual self. However, Althusser suggests that, 'If the whole is posed as *structured* i.e. as possessing a type of unity quite different from the type of unity of the spiritual whole, this is no longer the case' (p. 187; emphasis in original).

Structural causality is thus what Althusser calls a relation between a structure and its effects, between a structure and its subordinate structures. The structure is conceived as,

> a cause immanent in its effects in the Spinozist sense of the term, that *the whole existence of the structure consists of its effects*, in short that the structure, which is merely a specific combination of its peculiar elements is nothing outside its effects. (p. 189; emphasis in original)

Material existence of a structure is represented in Spinoza as the concept of an eternity, defined in the first part of Spinoza's *Ethic*, definition VIII as follows.

> By eternity, I understand existence itself, so far as it is conceived necessarily to follow from the definition alone of the eternal thing.
> *Explanation*—For such existence, like the essence of the thing, is conceived as an eternal truth. It cannot therefore be explained by duration or time, even if the duration be conceived without beginning or end.

Therefore, if the mode of production is conceived as a cause immanent in the effects, as an eternity, then the mode of production must be conceived as eternally reproducing the conditions of its own existence. That is to say, that given a Spinozist conception of mode of production as an eternity, what Althusser calls a relation of structural causality between a structure and its effects, between a structure and its subordinate structures, the capitalist mode of production, for example, reproduces its conditions of existence in subordinate (economic, political, ideological) structures, not as pure epiphenomena but as conditions of existence of the capitalist mode of production, *always*. Here, then, the status of the concept of reproduction is that of the mechanism of the *eternalization* of the mode of production. Althusser, however, also insists on the possibility of transition from one mode of production to another, though clearly at the cost of theoretical incoherence.

If the conditions of existence of a mode of production are produced as effects of that mode of production, then if relations of production specific to that mode of production are both the conditions of existence of that mode of production and the effects of that mode of production, then clearly transition is unthinkable. If we refer again to the essay 'Ideology and Ideological State Apparatuses' we find just this position in terms of the reproduction of relations of production being expanded by Althusser. It is clear that the possibility of transition is excluded since the mechanisms of the reproduction of relations of production always secures the eternal reproduction of the mode of production and the relations of production specific to the mode of production. On the other hand Althusser insists on the possibility of transition and on the effectivity of class struggle in transition. This insistence appears as an afterthought (see his P.S. to the ISA paper, Althusser, 1971, pp. 170—3) and can only be maintained at the cost of theoretical incoherence. Furthermore, in his P.S. Althusser retreats form his project of the elaboration of 'general theory'. His insistence on 'concrete' conditions and 'concrete' struggle allows him to insist on their effectivity but only at the cost of his general theory, his theory of ideology and his theoretical coherence.

Finally, the whole of his project for a general theory of ideology is predicated on the notion of the reproduction of relations of production in terms of the reproduction of relations between human subjects. However, since economic agents may take non-human forms such as joint-stock companies, religious orders etc., relations of production and hence their reproduction cannot be reduced to the reproduction of human subjects 'in ideology'.

Despite the theoretical problems in Althusser's work it has found its way into the sociology of education and into the work of Marxist educational theorists such as Paulo Freire. Let us examine the work of the latter.

## C. PAULO FREIRE AND THE PEDAGOGY OF THE OPPRESSED

Paulo Freire is a Brazilian educationalist and philosopher exiled after the military coup in 1964. In this chapter we are concerned with the theoretical concepts in Freire's discourse. There is no attempt to evaluate the practical educational work in the field of literacy and adult education, for which Paulo Freire is well known. His work is significant in the context of this book because it illustrates a number of *theoretical* problems which are associated with humanist and teleological[14] conceptions of transition to socialism found in certain variants of neo-Marxist theory. In addition, Freire's work is relevant to our earlier discussion of Young. Young insists that he uses the term political 'in Paulo Freire's sense that all action is political'.[15] There is however a more general case for an examination of Freire's writings. The latter are frequently cited by educationalists and theorists engaged in a wide range of forms of work. Writers in the field of adult education, for example, frequently make reference to his writings as do many sociologists of education in their attempts to criticize aspects of contemporary educational practice.[16]

Freire's writings are concerned with forms of 'cultural action' and, because many of the illustrations he uses in the elaboration of this concept refer to Latin American societies, there has been some debate as to the relevance of his work for a sociology of education in general.[17] I will argue that Freire's use of illustrations drawn from Latin American societies is, in itself, no grounds for the exclusion of his work from the sociology of education. Rather, it will be shown that in his work the central concept, the concept of the role of education in the transition to socialism, is theoretically incoherent.

In his references to Latin American societies Freire subscribes to the scheme elaborated in the work of Paul Baran and Paul Sweezy,[18] and subsequently in the work of André Gunder Frank.[19] Freire asserts that economic and *cultural* dominance is practised by a metropolitan society upon a dependent society. In Freire's adaptation of this scheme, however, there is an additional concept; for,

> If we consider *society as a being*, it is obvious that only a society which is a 'being-for-itself' can develop. Societies which are dual, 'reflex', invaded, and dependent on the metropolitan society cannot develop because they are alienated; their political, economic, and cultural decision-making power is located outside themselves, in the invader society. In the last analysis, the latter determines the destiny of the former. (Freire, 1972a, p. 130; emphasis added)

Our concern, here, is not to examine the schemes elaborated in the works of Baran and Sweezy or Frank,[20] but to establish the precise theoretical character of Freire's discourse. We are told that the forms of economic and cultural domination, with which his discourse is concerned, are not restricted to what is practised by a metropolitan society upon a dependent society. Freire maintains that forms of economic and *cultural* domination 'may be implicit in the domination of one class over another within the same society' (Freire, 1972a, p. 122). It might appear that Freire's discourse is concerned with *class* relations within societies in general, and is not restricted to 'metropolitan–dependent' relations of specific Latin American societies, and that since education is a major concern of his work, his theory is relevant to sociology of education generally. Such a conclusion would be without foundation, for the predominant concern of Freire's discourse is neither 'class societies' generally nor the specific societies of Latin America, but 'man' and the actions of man. Freire has a concept of society only in that it is a 'being', and society and social change only occurs in that it is a construction of the actions of man. Freire argues that man's historical task is the transformation of reality, which is precisely the *transformation of himself*, because in Freire's conception reality is constituted by men. The existence or the transformation of society is unthinkable except in that it is the actions and acts of transformation of men. Society is a 'being'. It is a Super-Subject which manifests itself in the phenomena of the individual beings of men. 'Social change' manifests itself in transformations of *man*. The dominant concept in Freire's anthropology is the 'humanisation of man', but:

> Within history, in concrete, objective contexts, *both* humanisation and dehumanisation are possibilities for man as an uncomplete being conscious of his incompleteness. But while both humanisation and dehumanisation are real alternatives, *only the first is man's vocation*. This vocation is constantly negated, yet it is affirmed by that very negation. It is thwarted by injustice, exploitation, oppression, and the violence of the oppressors; it is affirmed by the yearning of the oppressed for freedom and justice, and by their struggle to recover their lost humanity. (ibid., p. 20; emphasis added)

For Freire the specific character of the 'oppressed' is defined by the state of their 'being'. He postulates a conception of a 'complete being', in comparison to which the oppressed are incomplete, not fully human beings. It is the will and *cultural action* of the oppressors which prevents the oppressed (and also the oppressors themselves) from achieving their historical vocation as fully human beings. Freire announces that it is the 'great humanistic and historical task of the oppressed to liberate themselves and their oppressors as well' (ibid., p. 21). For the moment, however, the oppressors dominate the construction of 'oppressive reality' and this cultural hegemony exercised by the oppressors ensures that the *consciousness* of the oppressed is not liberated. It is this condition, specifically, which defines them as incomplete human beings *alienated* from the state of being fully human.

But all is not lost, for such circumstances are in direct default of man's 'ontological and historical vocation' (ibid., p. 31). 'History' merely *appears* to present the choice of humanization and dehumanization when there is no choice to be made, for it is part of the inevitable history of man that he fulfils his vocation to be fully human. The state of alienation of human beings is a *distortion* of this vocation, a temporal change of shape but not a breach of continuity in the process of the humanization of man.

The distortion of the ontological and historical vocation of man in which the oppressors enforce the state of alienation of the oppressed, occurs through the cultural action of the construction of 'oppressive reality'. The latter absorbs those within it and acts to submerge mens' consciousnesses. However, as we shall see, some human consciousnesses are able to transcend this submersion in oppressive reality, according to Freire. A crucial component in the construction of oppressive reality is 'anti-dialogical cultural action' which characterizes the action of the agents engaged in the educational 'processing' of the oppressed. Education plays a crucial role in the maintenance of the oppressed as alienated beings. Anti-dialogical cultural action in the educational system is characterized by the 'banking-concept' of education which is fundamental to the 'culture of silence' in which the oppressed are constrained to achieve the incomplete consciousness which characterizes their state of alienation.

The banking-concept of education entails anti-dialogical action in that it prevents dialogue, and education takes the form of the 'depositing' of information into the brains of those being 'educated'. The students are the 'depositories', the teachers the 'depositors' and education is the process of depositing—hence the term the 'banking-concept' of education.[21] Such is Freire's critique of the educational process. It is confined to an analysis of the interpersonal relations between teacher and student, which are alleged to entail a form of cultural action on the part of the oppressors characterized by 'narration'. Freire conceives the narrative process as an instrument of oppression in which the teachers are either conscious or unconscious agents of the oppressive process. His argument is that forms of cultural action, and specifically education as a form of cultural action, secures the conditions of existence of a form of consciousness in the oppressed through the construction of an oppressive reality in which the latter are absorbed. This maintenance of the relations of oppression between the oppressors and the oppressed is effected by:

> the historical-cultural configuration which we have called the 'culture of silence'. This mode of culture is a superstructural expression which conditions a special form of consciousness. The culture of silence 'overdetermines' the infrastructure in which it originates, as Althusser shows. (ibid., p. 57)

Freire, here, refers to the 'Althusserian' concept of 'structural causality'. However, Althusser is able to argue such a concept, and also posit a theory of transition, only at the cost of his theoretical coherence, and theoretical problems of a similar nature arise in Freire's discourse. If cultural action affects consciousnesses so that the state of being of man remains one of alienation, then the transformation of the consciousness of man, which the ontological and historical vocation of man 'necessitates', in Freire's teleological conception of humanization, is impossible. Freire is able to posit a conception of the 'humanisation of man' only at the cost of his theoretical coherence.

Freire proposes a theory of the transformation of the consciousness of man from his condition of alienation to a condition of 'freedom', and the latter is characterized by man in the state of being fully human and as such possessing a 'critical consciousness'. Freire proposes a theory of *cultural* revolution, in which education plays a crucial role. In this cultural revolution antidialogical cultural action is replaced by dialogical cultural action in a process of conscientization (conscientização).[22] The cultural revolution is preceded by a process of dialogical cultural action which occurs during the pre-revolutionary era. The move towards human transformation is the outcome of a *cultural struggle*; a struggle between forms of cultural action.

Cultural struggle is possible in Freire's conception only because certain cultural forms are able to transcend the dominant 'culture of silence'; their origin is beyond the realm of anything we can know. The crucial role in this cultural struggle is played by what Freire calls 'revolutionary leaders', who are the source of the cultural action which challenges the dominant culture. The revolutionary leaders' aim is for freedom and in their pedagogic practice they challenge the culture of silence, advancing dialogical cultural action and thus liberating the consciousness of the oppressed. In the pre-revolutionary era people

> are living in corpses, shadows of human beings, hopeless men, women and children victimized by an endless invisible war in which their remnants of life are devoured by tuberculosis, schistosomiasis, infant diarrhoea . . . by the myriad diseases of poverty. (Freire, 1972b, p. 139)

The achievement of the cultural revolution is that they are no longer shadows of human beings but fully conscious of their state of being. This could not have been achieved without cultural action on the part of the revolutionary leaders who have many of the properties of Max Weber's 'charismatic leaders' in that they are the *source* of that which challenges the dominant culture, the 'charismatic belief [which] revolutionises men "from within" and shapes material and social conditions according to its revolutionary will'.[23]

The ontological and historical vocation of men, then, is subject to the condition that there are 'revolutionary leaders', but furthermore they must be *radicals*, committed to human liberation. Radicalism, for Freire, is a question of attitudes and commitments of radicals. Freire is a radical whose programme is cultural action for freedom and the form it takes is the pedagogy of the oppressed. For Freire politics takes the form of *cultural action*. The pedagogy of the oppressed is an instrument for the critical discovery that both the oppressors and the oppressed are manifestations of dehumanization. The process of the humanization of all men supersedes oppressor and oppressed and all are free, fully human, no longer alienated shadows of the beings they were *intended to be*. In Freire's teleological conception of man, cultural action appears necessary because other forms of cultural action are holding back the forces of history. These forms act in the interests of the oppressors and their dominant form is active in contemporary educational systems.

> Pedagogy which begins with the egoistic interests of the oppressors (an egoism cloaked in the false generosity of paternalism) and makes of the oppressed the objects of its humanitarianism, itself *maintains and embodies* oppression. *It is an instrument* of dehumanization. (Freire 1972a, p. 30; emphasis added)

For this reason the pedagogy of the oppressed cannot be developed or practised by the oppressors (represented as they are by their agents the teachers), for it would be a 'contradiction in terms if the oppressors not only defended but actually implemented a liberating education' (ibid., p. 30). The crux of the problem Freire tells us is this:

> if the implementation of a liberating education requires *political power* and the oppressed have none, how then is it possible to carry out the pedagogy of the oppressed prior to the revolution? (ibid., p. 30)

Freire tells us that this is a question of the greatest importance and that one aspect of the reply is to be found in the distinction between *systematic education*, which can only be changed by political power, and *educational projects*, which should be carried out *with* the oppressed in the process of organizing them.

> The pedagogy of the oppressed, as a humanist and libertarian pedagogy, has two stages . . . In both stages it is always through action in depth that the culture of domination is *culturally* confronted. In the first stage this confrontation occurs through the change in the way the oppressed *perceive the world* of oppression; in the second stage, through the expulsion of the myths created and developed in the older order, which like spectres haunt

the new structure emerging from the revolutionary transformation. (ibid., p. 31; emphasis added)

Thus, in the period prior to transformation and in the revolutionary period as such, the mode of action which is to achieve transformation is cultural confrontation. Transformation is the outcome of cultural action and a crucial form of cultural action is educational projects. These are possible because certain individuals, the revolutionary leaders, are able to transcend cultural determinants. Freire argues both that culture is determinant and dominant, and that there are culturally transcendent subjects. These are his radical revolutionary leaders, who are the motive force of the history of man. But it is a history that has its *own* motive force, for it is man's ontological and historical vocation to be fully human. Freire's radicals are not strictly necessary, they are merely the materialized phenomena of an essential and spiritual process; the teleological process of the humanization of man.

Since M. F. D. Young subscribes to Freire's concept of politics, he subscribes to a concept which denegates the effectivity of political struggle. For Freire, politics is reduced to the cultural actions of radicals who are none the less redundant, because 'history' has its own motive force in relation to which they and their action are merely epiphenomenal; the epiphenomena of a necessary and inevitable process of the history of man.

## CONCLUSIONS

In this chapter we have examined and criticized a number of Marxist and neo-Marxist theoretical concepts, and in particular their elaboration in the works of Althusser and Freire. We have argued that despite the theoretical problems which are evident in Marxist and neo-Marxist theory, certain concepts[24] have been utilized uncritically in some branches of contemporary sociology of education. The problems inherent in Marxist and neo-Marxist theory mean that educational theory and policy cannot simply be deduced from the 'basic concepts' of Marxist and neo-Marxist discourse. This means that the work of contemporary analysis, theoretical development, educational policy formulation, and work on the issue of the role of education in the struggle for socialism remains the object of continuing labour.

# 4 Libertarianism and Sociology of Education

This chapter examines Ivan D. Illich's influential and much quoted *Deschooling Society*. Illich's book warrants examination here, firstly in its own right and secondly because it is frequently favourably referred to in the sociology of education. Furthermore, Illich's work forms one of the bases from which Bowles and Gintis attempt to elaborate a 'political economy' of education. As we shall see in the following chapter Bowles and Gintis are concerned, as are Parsons and Althusser, with relations between education and economy. Bowles and Gintis are concerned to develop a radical critique of Illich's *Deschooling Society* and on the basis of that critique to develop a political economy of education. [1]

Libertarian doctrines are hardly new to educational theory nor are they exclusive to the work of Illich. Nevertheless, his work has become something of a classic in radical/libertarian educational theory. Illich, however, refers to himself not as a libertarian but as a radical and a revolutionary. We shall see that the latter designation is spurious in that his revolution is impossible within the terms of his own theoretical discourse.

Illich's work has had a significant influence on the sociology of education in Britain as well as on educational theory generally. As we have already seen, M. F. D. Young is a radical sociologist and educational theorist who is concerned to develop educational alternatives. Young specifically argues that it is the task of a politics of educational knowledge to construct 'possible alternative models reflecting different assumptions about knowledge, learning and ability' (Young, 1972, p. 210). This task is directly based on the assumption that educational knowledge is an expression of the political priorities of those in a position to 'socially approve' knowledge, and by that process impose their meanings on the 'less powerful'. Young suggests that the new sociology be concerned with developing alternatives which are based on a rejection of established political characteristics in what counts as educational knowledge, and he indicates what these alternatives might be when he suggests that;

. . . it becomes necessary to question what is taken for granted in most educational practice, writing and research. This is not only that 'schooling is good', but that 'we all know what a good school is'. It is through starting from the opposite assumption 'that all schooling as we know it is harmful' that Illich (in *Deschooling Society*) is able to raise fundamental questions about the 'political' character of contemporary education. (Young, 1972, p. 205)

There is more than a passing reference to de-schooling in Young's work. It is a consequence of his rejection of any valid educational knowledge and the insistence on the conception of knowledge as a product of everyday experience (which is to be seen as of intrinsic value to the experiencing human subject in itself), that in order to be valid, educational knowledges must refer to these experiences themselves as their prior concern. This conception opens the way to the many 'radical alternatives', which prevail in educational theory and policy making, in the form of the so-called 'free-schooling', 'de-schooling' and 'community school projects'.[2] These latter conceptions insist on the primacy of the subjective meanings of pupils; the constructs of common-sense experiencing in everyday life. Young's rejection of educational knowledge because it is political in character leads to its rejection in favour of everyday experiences. Young claims that by assuming that established education is 'harmful' Illich is able to raise questions about the political character of contemporary education, and offer 'radical' alternatives. It will be argued here that, as with Young, Illich is able to do neither, that his position in *Deschooling Society* is little more than assertion, and that his politics are founded on a conceptualization which renders impossible the social and political change which is the object of his discourse.

## (i) ILLICH'S CONCEPTION OF 'SCHOOLING'

Young correctly points out that Illich considers that all schooling as we know it is harmful. Making a distinction between learning or education and 'schooling which goes on in institutions' and which he contends is 'publicly prescribed learning', Illich argues that

the mere existence of school discourages and disables the poor from taking control of their own learning. All over the world the school has an anti-educational effect on society: school is recognized as the institution which specializes in education. (Illich, 1971, p. 8)

Illich argues that education through schooling is a very costly, very complex, always arcane, and frequently almost impossible task, and precisely because it is recognized as the institution which specializes in education, school appropriates the money, manpower and goodwill available for education and in addition discourages other institutions from assuming educational tasks. He argues that universal education through schooling is not feasible economically and where it *is* undertaken schooling fails to educate, that is, it fails to promote 'real' learning. Furthermore, Illich considers schooling to be harmful in certain of its effects, in that,

> School has become the world religion of a modernized proletariat . . . the nation—state has adopted it, drafting all citizens into a graded curriculum leading to sequential diplomas not unlike the initiation rituals and hieratic promotions of former times. (p. 10)

Illich argues that the 'latent functions' performed by modern school systems are those of custodial care, selection, indoctrination and learning. The school is a modern institution which has as its primary purpose the 'shaping of man's vision of reality'. The agent of this process is the schoolteacher, who fuses in his person 'the functions of judge, ideologue and doctor', and the political interests of 'consumer society' are promoted in the 'hidden curriculum of schooling', that is, the 'ceremonial or ritual of schooling itself'.

Illich conceives educational systems as agencies whose function is the imposition of 'reality', that is, the imposition of meanings which *impose* a specific reality on the human consciousness. For Illich such meanings are the political interests of 'consumer society'. However, he also argues that the consciousness of human subjects is essentially free. Indeed, in Illich's conception, social, political and economic change is possible only because man is essentially free. How then is it possible, within Illich's conceptualization, to posit the possibility of other agents imposing on the consciousness of an essentially free human subjectivity? This question is of major importance because it is against this imposition that Illich's critique of modern educational institutions is directed.

Illich conceives of each human individual as a personally responsible being. If the imposition of the political interests of others is to be conceived of as possible, then each human individual must (of his own free will) be personally responsible for remaining unfree; that is, personally responsible for the imposition on the consciousness of his essentially free human subjectivity. In Illich's conception social, political and economic change presupposes that human individuals are *aware* of their essential freedom. However, the question remains that if individuals are not aware of their essential freedom, how is the state of unawareness brought about? Is it by choice or by imposition? If it is by choice, then human subjects must be conceived of as *choosing* to have meanings imposed on their consciousnesses. On the other hand, if it is, as Illich argues, that such institutions as education *impose* on human subjects the choices they make, then we are returned once again to the question of how it is possible to impose on the consciousness of an essentially free human subjectivity.

Illich's position is fundamentally incoherent since he insists on maintaining two logically incompatible positions. If man is essentially free his consciousness cannot be shaped or imposed on, if his consciousness can be shaped or imposed on then he cannot be free. However, it is man's essential freedom and his awareness of it which is the driving force of the institutional change which constitutes Illich's conception of social change.

## (ii)   THE 'INSTITUTIONAL SPECTRUM' AND SOCIAL CHANGE

The social system, in Illich's conceptualization, consists of a continuum of institutions. The 'institutional spectrum' runs from left to right, and Illich points out that his schema has nothing to do with the 'left-right spectrum used to characterise men and their ideologies' but rather that it characterizes social institutions and their *styles*. On the right of the institutional spectrum are the bureaucratic, manipulative institutions of which the schooling system is exemplary. The right-wing institutions have reached old age, and Illich's aim is their 'rejuvenation'. This rejuvenation constitutes Illich's conception of social change, and consists of the shifting of institutions from right to left along the institutional spectrum. The key to social transformation is the deschooling of society. Illich rejects what *he considers* to be the usual conception of the relationship between education and social structure and social change. He suggests that,

> We are used to considering schools as a variable, dependent on the political and economic structure. If we can change the style of political leadership, or promote the interests of one class or another, or switch from private to public ownership of the means of production, we assume the school system will change as well. (p. 73)

However, Illich argues that schools are fundamentally alike in all countries, be they fascist, democratic or socialist, big or small, rich or poor. In view of this identity, he argues that it is illusory to claim that schools are, in any profound sense, dependent variables and that 'to hope for fundamental change in the school system as an effect of conventionally conceived social or economic change is also an illusion' (p. 74). Illich maintains that he is a *radical* who 'hopes for fundamental change'. Such change is to be achieved by shifting the right-wing institutions over to the left of the institutional spectrum. The left and right wings of the spectrum are characterized as follows. On the right are found the 'most influential modern institutions' and these, are 'manipulative' institutions[3] which are either socially or psychologically 'addictive'. Illich argues that they invite compulsively repetitive use and frustrate alternative ways of achieving similar results. Their clearest example is the schools. On the left of the spectrum and opposed to the dominant manipulative institutions, Illich finds that the other type also exist, but only precariously. They are the 'convivial'[4] institutions which are the 'models for a more desirable future' (p. 53).

Radical social change involves a leftward shift along the institutional spectrum and it is argued that 'a political programme which does not explicitly recognise the need for deschooling is not revolutionary'. Illich maintains that he *is* revolutionary and he argues that the analysis of institutions according to their present placement on the left—right continuum enables him to clarify his belief that;

> *fundamental social change* must begin with a *change of consciousness* about institutions, and to explain why the dimension of a viable future turns on the rejuvenation of institutional style (p. 61; emphasis added)

Thus, the object of Illich's radical revolutionary politics is institutional *style*, and the mechanism of change of this style is the change of human consciousness. We need only know precisely what facilitates this change of human consciousness to complete the Illichian concept of politics. It is clear that whilst human consciousness is controlled by the manipulative institutions which dominate men and society, one thing remains outside their effectivity. The latter is a sphere of human freedom. It is this realm of free human subjectivity which facilitates the determined consciousness to change itself. Illich's position is, as we have argued above and is evident here, fundamentally incoherent since he insists on maintaining two logically incompatible positions. Illich's concept of politics which aims to rejuvenate institutions is therefore fundamentally incoherent. Politics presupposes precisely the change of consciousness which is rendered impossible in Illich's conception of the effectivity of the manipulative institutions.

The elaboration of the educational institution in *Deschooling Society* is much more than the elaboration of a mere example of a right-wing institution, and the deschooling of society has much wider ramifications in Illich's system than the mere rejuvenation of schooling. *Deschooling Society* is a radical's revolutionary political programme and although, as Illich agrees, it is a programme without a party, it is against schooling that the major thrust must be made against the prevailing social, political and economic order. This is because schooling is the most established and all-pervasive of the manipulative institutions. Illich argues,

> school touches us so intimately that none of us can expect to be liberated from it by something else. . . . Each of us is *personally responsible* for his or her *own deschooling*, and only we have the power to do it . . . (p. 47; emphasis added)

It is now clear why deschooling is a programme without a party. In Illich's conception politics is reduced to *individual* consciousness and political action is the *individual act* of becoming aware of the essential freedom of man. As we have already seen, however, it is precisely this individual act which Illich is unable to theorize coherently because his elaboration of its concept involves him in the maintenance of two logically incompatible positions. Nevertheless, Illich is content to base his concept of politics and political action on logically incompatible concepts of the human essence, and to posit man's personal responsibility as the motive force of social, political and economic change. Thus, the responsibility of the free personality is the sphere in which the initial break is made by the otherwise institutionally *determined* human consciousness, and this leads to fundamental change. Human freedom exists externally to the social system, but it is the motive force of political, economic and social change. That Illich does indeed endow the sphere of human freedom with metaphysical powers can be seen in his assertion that having initiated the shift in consciousness which leads to the shift in specular position of the educational institutions from right to left, the resultant deschooling,

> would endanger the survival not only of the *economic order* built on the coproduction of goods and demands, but equally of the *political order* built on the nation–state into which students are delivered by the school. (p. 49; emphasis added)

In conclusion we should note that the operational problems of the 'convivial' left institutions of the deschooled society need not concern us here.[5] For they 'are meant to serve a society *which does not now exist*' (p. 73). The convivial institutions of a deschooled society, like the politics that would lead us there, are but the dreams of a priest. The combination of the sociological speculation which M. F. D. Young insists that our new sociologists in educational research should engage in, and the dreams of a radical priest can be no serious advance for the sociology of education. The attempt to 'construct possible alternative models reflecting different assumptions about knowledge, learning and ability' which is, according to Young, a major aim of the politics of educational knowledge, cannot be successfully undertaken by reference to the work of Ivan Illich, and contrary to Young's expectations that Illich is able to raise fundamental questions about the political character of education, the reference to Illich merely plunges the concept into even deeper confusion.

# 5 The 'Political Economy' of Education in the work of Bowles and Gintis

We have already seen that in the work of Talcott Parsons and Louis Althusser relations between the economy and the education system play a significant role in their contribution to educational theory. The work of Samuel Bowles and Herbert Gintis, collected together in their book *Schooling in Capitalist America*, is concerned explicitly with the development of a 'political economy' of education in capitalist societies. This chapter examines the central theoretical arguments in Bowles and Gintis' attempt to establish the relations between the economy and the educational system.

In the introduction to the present book it was argued that one of its objects was to examine and to distinguish between radical and Marxist theories of education. Bowles and Gintis, on the other hand, are concerned with distinguishing between certain forms of radicalism (e.g. Illich's radicalism) and their own critique of schooling in capitalist society, in order to establish the radical character of their own theory which they refer to as both Marxist and radical. Now, we are not concerned, here, with the labels which writers attach to themselves and to their work. Bowles and Gintis claim to have been influenced by Marxist writers and their work is littered with quotations from and references to Marxist writings.

The theoretical concepts which appear in Bowles and Gintis' work diverge considerably from Marxist theory but they, nevertheless, refer to their own work as Marxian theory of the educational system in advanced capitalist societies. Now, just as we are not concerned with the labels which writers attach to their work, neither are we concerned with the divergence of discourse from its supposed theoretical foundation as the basis of its criticism. It is not the object of this chapter to criticize the work of Bowles and Gintis in terms of its divergence from the 'basic concepts' of classical Marxism, or indeed any other variant of Marxist discourse, but in terms of the internal logic and the relations between concepts within their own discourse.

The book *Schooling in Capitalist America* was written over a period of seven years and many sections of it are either rewritings of earlier articles or schematic accounts of arguments which appear in more theoretical detail elsewhere. In chapter 10 of their book, for example, Bowles and Gintis examine the work of Illich. This examination is a schematic account of the more theoretically elaborated critique of Illich titled 'Towards a Political Economy of Education: A Radical Critique of Ivan Illich's *Deschooling Society*' which appeared in the *Harvard Educational Review*.[1] This latter article goes beyond a critique of Illich and attempts to develop the notion of a political economy of education. In this chapter criticism of the work of Bowles and Gintis will be levelled at their more theoretically elaborate accounts so that in examining their critique of Illich we will refer to the article in the *Harvard Educational Review*. We will discuss Bowles and Gintis' critique of Illich by way of proceeding to an examination of their conception of the political economy of education in that article, in other articles and in *Schooling in Capitalist America*.

Much of *Schooling in Capitalist America* is rambling and polemical. There are, however, a number of central and recurring themes. These form the basis of a 'general theory' of education in capitalist society. This general theory is derived from what Bowles and Gintis suppose to be the quintessential capitalist society—the United States of America. In this chapter, we are concerned with neither the 'validity' of their analysis of education in American capitalist society, nor with relations between a general theory and other 'real' societies (Britain, France, Germany, etc.) but with the internal logic of their argument.

For Bowles and Gintis, in capitalist society education functions as an agency of supply of 'appropriately' educated manpower to the economy. There are two modes of appropriateness of the characteristics of manpower supplied by the education system. Firstly, the education system releases differentiated manpower to the economy. That is, educated manpower, or labour, is released at appropriate stages of its development; at different ages, after different lengths of training and with different technical capacities and qualifications. The educated labour, or manpower, supplied by the education system is differentiated according to, and in a way which is appropriate to, the 'needs' of the economy and specifically the different levels of the work processes within the economy.

The educated manpower supplied to the economy by the education system has another mode of 'appropriateness'; it is appropriately 'alienated'. Capitalist economies both 'need' and produce an 'alienated' work force. For Bowles and Gintis, the conditions to which workers are subjected in capitalist production processes are inimical to the realization of the 'essential' character of human labour.[2] This inimicality has two consequences. On the one hand, workers are 'alienated' or estranged from their essential human character as an effect of capitalist production processes. On the other, labour is seen as continually seeking to subvert these production processes and an object of capitalist enterprise calculation is to prevent such subversion.[3]

The education system in capitalist societies makes an intervention in the consciousness of labour on behalf of the capitalist enterprise and the production processes of capitalism by 'pre-alienating' the consciousness of future labour (children and youth). The education system functions to assist the capitalist enterprise in its object of prevention of the subversion of the production processes of capitalism. In effect the prevention of the subversion of capitalist production processes is secured by a unitary/organizing/calculating spiritual entity—capitalism. Relations of production are conceived as relations between human subjective consciousnesses[4] in the production process. The reproduction of the relations of production, which is the function of the education system in capitalist societies, is the reproduction of the alienated consciousness of future labour or manpower.

The relations between the economy and the education system are 'overseen' and 'legitimated' by an ideology called 'IQism'. Thus, appropriately alienated consciousnesses are secured in individuals, and individuals are differentiated and distributed to the economy and the various levels of the production processes of the capitalist economy. Individuals recognize their positions in the production processes of the capitalist economy as legitimate and appropriate as a function of the ideology of IQism.

The object of the present chapter is not to show that Bowles and Gintis' assertions are 'true' or 'false' in particular empirical cases, but to demonstrate that they have no coherent *theoretical* foundation.

## (i) THE RADICAL CRITIQUE OF ILLICH'S *DESCHOOLING SOCIETY*

We have already seen that Illich is a radical. Herbert Gintis is concerned to develop a radical critique of Illich's arguments on schooling in capitalist society and to go beyond that critique to develop a 'political economy' of education in capitalist societies. In his paper, 'Towards a Political Economy of Education: A Radical Critique of Ivan Illich's *Deschooling Society*'[5] Gintis argues that Illich's critique of schooling is not entirely unsuccessful but that 'his analysis is incomplete'. The 'strengths of Illich's analysis lie in his consistent and pervasive methodology of negation. . . . Illich's failures can be consistently traced to his refusal to pass *beyond* negations' (p. 94).

Only in one sphere does he go beyond negation, and this is his major contribution. While technology is in fact dehumanizing (thesis), he does *not* reject technology (antithesis). Rather, he goes beyond technology *and* its negation towards a schema of liberating technological forms in education. (p. 95)

We have already seen in the previous chapter, however, that in Illich's own conception transition to a society in which such forms are possible and appropriate is impossible. Since Illich does not provide the means to 'go beyond' present institutions even Gintis' limited praise is somewhat generous.

An index of Illich's failure to go 'beyond negations' according to Gintis, is that 'Illich rejects politics in favor of individual liberation'. Furthermore, 'he affirms the *laissez-faire* capitalist model and its core institutions; in rejecting schools, Illich embraces a commodity-fetishist cafeteria-smorgasbord ideal in education; and in rejecting political action, he affirms a utilitarian individualistic conception of humanity' (p. 95). For Gintis, however,

> The most serious lapse in Illich's analysis is his implicit postulation of a human 'essence' in all of us, preceding all social experience—potentially blossoming but repressed by manipulative institutions. (p. 95)

In the previous chapter we saw that there are fundamental theoretical problems with the Illichian conception of the economy, politics and schooling and the conception of the relations between them. The nub of the problem is how social change can be achieved in Illich's system. On the other hand Gintis argues that 'Illich's model of consumption-manipulation is crucial at every stage of his political argument. But it is substantially *incorrect*' (p. 75; emphasis added).

Before we examine the basis of Gintis' argument that Illich is 'incorrect' let us briefly examine the accuracy of his reading of Illich. Gintis describes Illich's conception of the institutional spectrum, for example, as consisting of the manipulative institutions and 'convivial' institutions. However, Gintis argues that in Illich's system the latter are associated 'with leftist political orientation' (p. 75). This is quite wrong. As we have already seen, Illich points out that his schema has nothing to do with the 'left–right spectrum used to characterise men and their ideologies' (p. 53) and this self assessment is substantially accurate.

Mis-representation apart, Gintis' examination is based on an account of the 'incompleteness' of Illich's work and on an argument that it is 'wrong' because of its 'lapses'. Lapses *from* what? Incompleteness by comparison to what? Gintis' critique attempts to measure Illich against some unspecified ideal 'complete' conceptualization. As we saw in chapter 4, Illich's discourse is fundamentally incoherent; that is, it is incoherent at the crucial levels within his discourse. Illich's position is not one that could be rectified, as Gintis' critique implies, by filling in certain gaps, by making good certain lapses and 'completing' his account. No cosmetic treatment could rectify Illich's work because contrary to the implication that the problem is merely one of incompleteness, Illich's system is theoretically incoherent at a fundamental level. For example, Illich does *not* reject politics in favour of individual liberation (Gintis posits some ideal concept of 'politics' here it must be assumed), Illich's politics *is* individual liberation. It is, however, a form of politics which is impossible within Illich's own discourse.

The critique of Illich forms one of the bases for Bowles and Gintis' development of a 'political economy' of education. For Gintis, Illich's concern with consumption rather than with production is a major 'failing'. Gintis argues that 'to understand consumption in capitalist society requires a *production* orientation, in contrast to Illich's emphasis on 'institutionalized values' as basic explanatory variables' (p. 81; emphasis in the original). Gintis tells us that whereas Illich locates the source of social problems and value crises of modern societies in their need to reproduce alienated patterns of consumption, he (Gintis) argues that these patterns are merely manifestations of deeper workings of the economic system (p. 71). Laying the ground for a political economy of education which amounts to little more than a vulgar economism, Gintis tells us that,

> Illich locates the source of social decay in the autonomous, manipulative behavior of corporate bureaucracies. I shall argue, in contrast, that the source must be sought in the normal operation of the basic *economic* institutions of capitalism . . . (p. 76)

(ii) THE 'POLITICAL ECONOMY' OF EDUCATION IN CAPITALIST SOCIETIES

A recurrent theme of Bowles and Gintis' book *Schooling in Capitalist America* and in particular in their 'correspondence thesis' is the argument that,

> Different levels of education feed workers into different levels within the occupational structure and, correspondingly, tend toward an internal organization comparable to levels in the hierarchical division of labor. (p. 132)

This argument is functionalist. Education is treated as an agency of supply of educated manpower and it is argued that the internal organization of education is structured so as to be compatible with the 'needs' of industry. The theoretical bases of these arguments have been effectively demolished in an article not specifically directed at Bowles and Gintis titled 'The economy and the educational system in capitalist societies' by Athar Hussain.[6]

In the first part of Bowles and Gintis' argument education is treated as a supplier of educated manpower. However, as Hussain demonstrates, although educational qualifications serve as the bases of selection for occupations it is not the educational system which actually channels individuals into occupations (p. 419). On the contrary 'the volume, categories and the terms of employment are determined not inside but outside the educational system' (p. 419). The implication that the volume, categories and the terms of employment are determined inside the educational system, absurd as this notion is, nevertheless is part of Bowles and Gintis' 'correspondence thesis'. Their argument that education is a supplier of educated manpower to different levels within the occupational structure is dependent on the notion that educational qualifications (and differing levels of qualification) serve not only as criteria for selection to occupations but as entitlements to occupations. However, educational qualifications do not, by themselves, determine terms of employment or even employment as such. Furthermore, the educational system cannot allocate individuals to occupations that do not exist. Whilst Bowles and Gintis are concerned with the 'long shadow of employment' the problem for youth in Britain is more often the long shadow of unemployment. This brings us to the second part of the Bowles and Gintis argument.

Bowles and Gintis argue that there is a reciprocal relationship between education and the economy in capitalist society. In addition to education acting as supplier of educated manpower, the educational system in order to do so tends towards an internal organization comparable to levels in the hierarchical division of labour. In America for example,

> blacks and other minorities are concentrated in schools whose repressive, arbitrary, generally chaotic internal order, coercive authority structures, and minimal possibilities for advancement mirror the characteristics of inferior job situations. Similarly, predominantly working-class schools tend to emphasize behavioral control and rule-following, while schools in well-to-do suburbs employ relatively open systems that favor greater student participation, less direct supervision, more student electives, and, in general, a value system stressing internalized standards of control. (p. 132)

These different forms of internal organization of schooling reflect the forms of organization in the economy and thus fulfil its 'needs'.

One of the problems with this argument, irrespective of whether certain sections of industry really do require individuals with the form of training that they describe, is that Bowles and Gintis provide no mechanism by which the economy secures such forms. No mechanism, that is, except the 'normal' mechanism whereby the economy generates the economically poor and the rich, their schools and the practices in the schools. Now, whilst it is clear that economic factors influence the form of education that individuals receive,[7] though in a more complex fashion than Bowles and Gintis propose, it is not at all clear that this influence of the economy amounts to a strict form of control such that the economy secures its 'needs'.

In capitalist economies there is no strict mechanism of control of education to suit the 'needs' of the economy. One of the reasons is that at the level of economic planning practised in capitalist economies there is little or no basis for knowledge of the manpower requirements sufficiently in advance of those requirements on which to plan education and training. More importantly, however, educational institutions are limited in their ability to match the supply of labour with demand. 'This limit is imposed by the fact that it is left to students to decide which courses they follow and the educational institutions do not necessarily tailor the numbers entering different courses to the requirements of the labour market' (Hussain, 1976, p. 427).

Of course, in Bowles and Gintis' conceptualization, no mechanisms other than the 'normal operations' of the economy need be supposed. They argue that individuals do not have any choices over their education, and the poor in particular are forced from poverty into poor schools and so into low-paid occupations and poverty. The same mechanism applies to the working–class and the 'well-to-do' but at a different level of the socio-economic hierarchy.

Many of Bowles and Gintis' theoretical problems are related to their dogmatic assertions as to the determinant role of the economy in relations with the educational system. At the same time we have argued that the educational system is indeed powerless in the face of determination by the economy of the volume, categories and terms of employment. There is no contradiction here. Whilst Bowles and Gintis insist on the determinant role of the economy as an automatic mechanism we have insisted on the elaboration of mechanisms of the relations between education and the economy. The question of whether the economy or the educational system is the 'determinant' factor cannot be simply 'given'. On the contrary, the character of the relations between the educational system and the economy can only be established by definite theoretical and empirical research. This can be illustrated by reference to the issue of unemployment.

In his article Hussain distinguishes between two categories of unemployment, namely aggregate and structural unemployment. Aggregate unemployment refers to a situation where the total number of vacancies is less than the total number of unemployed. Here unemployment can only be reduced through the creation of more jobs and the educational system has no role to play in this. No amount of education can bridge the gap between unemployment and vacancies (Hussain, 1976, p. 427). One of the most pressing problems for youths leaving school in Britain is the gap between the number of unemployed, of which they are likely to be a part, and the number of vacancies. This is an economic problem. It is due to the volume of employment and this is determined outside the educational system, in the economy.

The second form of unemployment is structural unemployment. The latter refers to a situation where there is an overall balance between vacancies and unemployment but a lack of correspondence between the types of labour demanded and the types of labour supplied on the market. Structural unemployment results from the fact that the labour market is highly differentiated and there are spatial or regional differences as well as the distribution of ability or competence to perform different kinds of work (Hussain, 1976, p. 427).

Now, in this latter case the educational system does have a role to play and this role is not 'determined' by the economy in the sense that the educational system must perform its role in a specific way, or 'automatically'. Indeed, the educational system may not perform any role and in that case structural unemployment will remain so long as no other agency intervenes.[8] The educational system may play a role in alleviating structural unemployment in so far as it is due to mismatching between the skills and abilities demanded by employers and those which the unemployed possess. However, as Hussain argues, 'the efficacy of educational institutions depends on the range of vocational training provided in them and the extent to which competence for occupations is defined in terms of educational qualifications' (Hussain, 1976, p. 427). This limitation is additional to the limitation, already discussed, imposed by the fact that students are left to decide which courses they follow and educational institutions do not necessarily tailor their course numbers to the requirements of the labour market. In addition there are incalculable limitations of a cultural nature. For example, the reluctance of workers (young or old) to move from one region to another.

To summarize, what we have argued is that rather than the economy playing a determinat role *per se*, certain aspects of the relations between the educational system and the economy are determined by the economy, whilst other aspects are determined by the forms of organization of the educational system as such. The form of organization of the educational system cannot be conceived as a mere effect of the economy. The educational system has a number of conditions of existence, including political, legal and cultural and specific limitations on its form and modes of organization and operation. These limitations are not exclusively 'economic'. Education policy is part of social policy and as such it is subject to political control and political 'determination'.

There is no general theoretical basis for Bowles and Gintis' argument that in capitalist societies the educational system functions as an agency of supply of appropriately educated manpower. Bowles and Gintis do not provide coherent theory of the mechanisms of this alleged relationship between education and economy. That is, there is no coherent theory of the mechanisms whereby the economy is able to secure in the educational system conditions which constrain it to produce and supply manpower of appropriate levels of technical competence and qualification.

Bowles and Gintis argue that the educational system functions as an agency of supply of manpower which has another mode of 'appropriateness'—its 'alienated' character. They argue that the 'reproduction of the social relations of production depends on the reproduction of consciousness' (p. 127). They are specifically concerned with the alienated consciousness of the individual worker. Relations of production are conceived as relations between individual workers and capitalists or the 'capitalist class'. We need not repeat, here, the discussion of the consequences of the reduction of the concept of relations of production to relations between the consciousnesses of individuals. Let us examine other major aspects of Bowles and Gintis' argument in a little more detail.

The work processes of capitalist production are essentially alienating and the educational system functions to reproduce alienated consciousness appropriate to the 'needs of the capitalist class' and their profits.

> Forms of consciousness and behavior fostered by the educational system must themselves be alienated, in the sense that they conform neither to the dictates of technology in the struggle with nature, nor to the inherent developmental capacities of individuals, but rather to the needs of the capitalist class. It is the prerogatives of capital and the imperatives of profit, not human capacities and technical realities, which render U.S. schooling what it is. This is our charge. (pp. 130–1)

Thus, capitalism and the 'prerogatives of capital' are attributed an organizing and calculating capacity. Capitalism as an entity calculates its own 'needs' and organizes its own 'needs' in other non-economic institutions (e.g. the educational system) and thus secures the reproduction of alienated consciousness.

Of course, Gintis' critique of Illich includes the argument that Illich postulates a 'human essence in us all' and this is, according to Gintis, the most 'serious lapse' in Illich's analysis. Bowles and Gintis are explicitly opposed to Illich's essentialism but merely replace it with one of their own. Whereas for Illich the essence of human nature is repressed by the manipulative institutions and the 'need to reproduce alienated patterns of consumption', for Bowles and Gintis, human individuals are alienated from their essential human nature (the inherent developmental capacities of individuals) by the 'normal operation of the basic economic institutions of capitalism' and specifically by the 'prerogatives of capital and the imperatives of profit'.

For Bowles and Gintis the process of alienation, that is, the process of the 'self-estrangement' of individuals from their essential human nature, is a process which is itself part of the essential nature of 'capitalism'. 'Capitalism' is an essentially spiritual entity and it is this characteristic of its nature that allows it to intervene in other aspects of social life (e.g. education) and to secure its 'needs' without specific mechanisms. The general means through which capitalism is able to secure effects in other spheres of social life is *spiritual*. For Bowles and Gintis capitalism is an all-pervasive unitary/ organizing/calculating *spiritual* entity.

Bowles and Gintis' essentialism is evident, then, both at the level of their conception of 'capitalist society' and at the level of their conception of human individuals and their 'consciousness'. Their explicit hostility to essentialism is largely ornamental. That is, they mimic Marx's opposition to the conception of essential human nature in arguing that social life determines consciousness whilst at the same time arguing that social life alienates individuals and their consciousness from its essential human nature.

(iii)  THE CONCEPT OF THE 'LEGITIMATION FUNCTION' OF 'IQISM'

Bowles and Gintis argue that relations between the economy and the educational system in capitalist societies are 'legitimated' by an ideology which is called 'IQism'. We shall come to their definition of the notion of IQism in a moment. First a brief word on the uses of psychometric testing and its relationship to education in Britain and America.

In 1969 Professor Arthur Jensen published the paper 'How Much Can We Boost IQ and Scholastic Achievement?' in the *Harvard Educational Review*.[9] In it he insisted that individual differences in 'intelligence' are to a major extent genetically determined, and that some racial and social classes are genetically inferior to others in intellectual ability. In Britain the publication of similar arguments in Professor H. J. Eysenck's *Race, Intelligence and Education* sought to popularize such ideas. Eysenck and Jensen have been attacked by 'environmentalists' and by some sociologists of education who claim that IQ testing is 'unfair' because the results cannot be freed from 'cultural bias' in the tests. We shall return to those arguments in a moment. First, a brief note on the background to arguments about 'genetic inferiority'.

The notion of genetic and racial inferiority was a pronounced element of Victorian thought. In his book *Hereditary Genius* the psychologist Francis Galton says, 'It is in the most unqualified manner that I object to pretensions of natural equality', and he goes on to say that 'The mistakes that the Negroes made in their own matters were so childish, stupid and simpleton-like, as frequently to make me ashamed of my own species'. Galton is one of the founding fathers of intelligence testing and many of his followers including the mathematician Karl Pearson shared his beliefs. Jensen and Eysenck believe that black Americans are inferior intellectually to whites. They believe that the Irish are similarly inferior to the English, and the British working class to the middle class.[10]

The academic debate over notions of 'racial' and 'genetic' inferiority was reaching a crescendo at the time when the Nazis were using the hereditary view as a justification for genocide—their attempt to exterminate the Jews. As Liam Hudson points out: 'Once the war was over, and the atrocities of the death camps became public knowledge, the hereditary view (with certain geographical exceptions) became taboo. In South Africa, hereditary arguments were still used as the justification for apartheid, and in the southern states of America they were used to justify the social repression of the blacks. Elsewhere, such ideas were banished from public debate. Now they have resurfaced . . .'.[11]

Educationalists and others are concerned about the resurfacing of the hereditary view and notions about 'racial' and 'genetic' inferiority for many reasons, one of which is the consequence of such arguments for educational policy. In the USA the work of Jensen, and others who have produced similar results, has been presented to committees of Congress concerned with the formulation of domestic welfare policy. Jensen's article 'How Much Can We Boost IQ and Scholastic Achievement?' explicitly attacks Project Headstart which was a programme of 'compensatory education' designed to provide improved resources for under-privileged children. Jensen's argument is that such projects are doomed to failure because of the genetic inferiority of those whom the project was aimed to help. Hence it has been argued that taxpayers' money should not be wasted on the 'ineducable'.[12] In his excellent book *The Science and Politics of I.Q.*, Leon Kamin argues that,

> The I.Q. test in America, and the way in which we think about it, has been fostered by men committed to a particular social view. That view includes the belief that those on the bottom are genetically inferior victims of their own immutable defects. The consequence has been that the I.Q. test has served as an instrument of oppression against the poor—dressed in the trappings of science, rather than politics. The message of science is heard respectfully, particularly when the tidings it carries are soothing to the public conscience. There are few more soothing messages than those historically delivered by the I.Q. testers. The poor, the foreign-born, and racial minorities were shown to be stupid. They were shown to have been born that way. The underprivileged are today demonstrated to be ineducable, a message as soothing to the public purse as to the public conscience. (p. 2)

Psychometric testing was used in post-war Britain as a means of allocating individuals to different secondary schools within the tripartite system. The 1944 Education Act required local authorities to provide secondary education 'offering such variety of instruction and training as may be desirable in view of their different ages, abilities and aptitudes'. In the late 1940s and early 1950s, as they attempted to operate the Act, the proposals of Sir Cyril Norwood[13] and his associates became the officially accepted form of secondary school organization. As Gerald Bernbaum points out, these proposals

> suited the existing school buildings and gave point to the selective examination. In many districts there were few technical schools and the effective system was built round a few grammar schools and a large number of secondary modern schools. Nationally, only about 20 per cent of the age group could enter grammar schools each year. Because of the growing number of children taking the examination known as the 11 + and the removal of the opportunity of parents to pay fees to achieve grammar school places for their children, the arrangements for choosing that 20 per cent became a matter for public and national debate by the mid-1950s.[14]

In the 1950s and the early 1960s certain educationalists began to question and criticize the arrangements for selection of children at the age of 11 + and in particular the psychometric tests. It was these arguments and attendant arguments against 'social injustice' and for 'equality of opportunity' and for 'fairness' which, together with the political force of the Labour Party, brought about the moves against psychometric testing and the moves towards the implementation of a comprehensive system of schooling. Of course, just as there are few sociologists who would deny the existence of individual human differences, there are few psychologists who would deny the importance of social and cultural factors in the determination of the conditions of the social patterns of educational achievement. For this and for other reasons concerned with the nature of psychometry itself many psychologists (e.g. Tort, 1977; Hudson, 1972) reject the validity of psychometric testing and the segregation of children according to alleged intelligence, and support the moves towards comprehensive schooling. Many writers, including sociologists and psychologists of education, argue that psychometric testing was itself a major instrument in the allocation of educational resources and that the resultant distribution of resources was a major source of differential educational opportunity and achievement.

This latter argument was often coupled with further arguments as to the validity of psychometric testing as such. These arguments took various forms. For example, some commentators stressed the persistent lack of any means of determining the relative importance of 'innate intelligence' in relation to other factors (which were also admitted to be of significance) in the psychometric tests' resultant 'measured intelligence'. That is, what part of 'measured intelligence' was 'innate intelligence' and how much was the result of other factors, and how could the relative importance of each be determined?

One of these 'other factors' was said to be culture, and some critics of psychometric testing argued that tests involved 'cultural bias' no matter how much the psychometricians attempted to adjust the procedures of their tests to eliminate such bias. These critics implicitly accept the validity of psychometric tests but argue that in practice it is not possible to rule out forms of bias. This mode of argument is sometimes referred to as the 'libertarian view' or the 'environmentalist view' and it advances a sociologistic critique of IQ testing.

In the sociologistic critique of IQ testing (a critique often advanced both by sociologists and psychologists) it is argued that IQ tests do measure real differences between individuals but that these measures are not measures which are attributable solely to innate intelligence. It is usually argued that the scores on IQ tests are influenced by 'environment' or more specifically by 'cultural differences'. In that this position is most often taken by educationalists who are concerned to combat the harmful effects of educational practices based on IQ testing it is, in the most part, taken up by well-meaning people.

The 'environmental view', laudable as it may appear, is based on the premise that there *is* such a thing as 'innate intelligence' but that this can never be measured because there is no *means* of determining the relative importance of 'innate intelligence' and 'environmental' or 'learned' factors.

One problem with this argument is that it appears to leave open the idea that with further 'scientific' labour—for the psychometrician the production of more sophisticated psychometric techniques—it might be possible to determine the relative importance of different factors. Such a notion is untenable because it is based on the influential but confused idea of 'genetically determined potential ability' (a notion which is also implicit in the commonly expressed idea of 'wasted ability') and on the notion that it is separable from actual behaviour.

As Joanna Ryan argues in her article 'IQ—The Illusion of Objectivity',[15] the notion of genetically determined potential ability 'involves the notion of ability that is characteristic of an individual prior to any interaction with the environment, and thus independent of any social or specific educational influences' (p. 41). The problem with the notion, and the reason why no amount of 'scientific' labour can provide the means of measurement of genetically determined potential is that 'potential' is necessarily expressed in actual behaviour. As Ryan says, 'the notion of potential ability both as something abstracted from all interactions with the environment and at the same time as something measurable in a person's behaviour simply does not make sense' (p. 42). Clearly, the prior issue is not that of the *means* of measurement but of the conception of the existence in isolation of what it is that is supposed to be measured.

In their functionalist analysis of relations between the educational system and the economy Bowles, Gintis and Meyer[16] assert that

The educational system legitimates economic inequality by providing an ostensibly open, objective and meritocratic mechanism for assigning individuals to unequal economic positions. Indeed, the more meritocratic the educational process appears, the better it serves to legitimate inequality. (p. 234)

'Legitimation' is defined by Bowles and Gintis as 'the fostering of a generalized consciousness among individuals which prevents the formation of the social bonds and critical understanding whereby existing social conditions might be transformed' (Bowles and Gintis, 1976 p. 104). The legitimation function of education can be seen in the major aspects of the education process and in particular in the practices of screening by IQ and cognitive test scores, in tracking and in emphasis on competitive examinations and grading. It is argued that 'beneath the facade of meritocracy lies the reality of an educational system geared towards the reproduction of a class structure quite unrelated to technical requirements and efficiency standards' (Bowles, Gintis and Meyer, 1975–6, p. 235). One of the main illustrations of their thesis is 'the recent IQ debate'. Bowles, Gintis and Meyer see the notion of IQ as performing a 'legitimation function'. Let us examine their argument.

Bowles and Gintis define 'IQism' as 'the IQ theory of social inequality' (Bowles and Gintis, 1976, p. 119). They represent IQism as a theory of social and economic inequality which argues that such inequality is a function of either or both 'environmental IQ' and 'genetic IQ'. They oppose IQism mainly because they are opposed to its alleged effects—its legitimation function. Their opposition is developed by an argument *not* against the concept of IQ as such but against the 'theory of IQism'. The result is that despite their bitter opposition to IQism and their attack on other critics who 'blandly accept' the 'validity of the genetic school's description of the social function of intelligence' (Bowles, Gintis and Meyer, 1975–6, p. 257), they themselves leave the concept of IQ *per se* untouched. Indeed, in taking up the argument in the form they do they implicitly accept the *concept* of IQ. Bowles, Gintis and Meyer summarize their position as follows:

the proponent of IQism argues that higher social class (or race) is associated with a higher IQ, which in turn leads to a greater chance of economic success. We shall show, however, that this inference is simply erroneous. Specifically, we will demonstrate the truth of the following proposition: *the fact that economic success tends to run in the family arises almost completely independently from any inheritance of IQ; genetic or environmental.* (p. 258; emphasis in the original)

This proposition is 'demonstrated' by 'our statistical technique' of 'linear regression analysis'. The techniques of linear regression analysis are only hinted at in *Schooling in Capitalist America* and in the paper 'Education, IQ, and the Legitimation of the Social Division of Labor' but they nevertheless allow Bowles, Gintis and Meyer to produce statistical 'evidence' to 'prove' their case. Their demonstration that 'the lack of importance of the specifically genetic mechanism operating via IQ in the intergenerational reproduction of economic inequality is even more striking' than the fact that 'statistical association between family background and income is hardly affected by holding childhood IQ constant', is dependent on and 'assumes that all direct influences of socio-economic background and income have been eliminated, and that the non-cognitive components of schooling's contribution to economic success are eliminated as well' (Bowles, Gintis and Meyer, 1975–6, p. 260).

Unfortunately for the reader of *Schooling in Capitalist America* and other papers by Bowles and Gintis and their associates, the means of 'holding constant' certain factors and eliminating others remains somewhat tenuous to say the least. However, it is not the intention of the present author to engage in a critique of statistical techniques and methods. Rather, it is argued, here, that there is no basis to arguments over the statistics on IQ because a coherent concept of IQ as such cannot be sustained. If the concept of IQ as such cannot be sustained then arguments about the relative importance of IQ by comparison to 'other factors' must be vacuous.

In as much as it has quantifiable meaning at all the notion of 'intelligence' as such is expressed in terms of a quotient, 'IQ'. The notion of IQ (intelligence quotient) has no meaning outside the means of its measurement. That is, there is no meaning to the notion of IQ outside or independent of the IQ test.

Psychometric testing involves the assigning of numerical values to behaviour or performance in tests such that differences in behaviour or performance can be represented by differences in score. The notion of such a test assumes that the operational procedures of the test can be structured so as to produce a scale of numerical values. Differences in score are represented in the form of a scale. When a succession of similar operations can be performed on a succession of similar objects with each different result being assigned a different number value, the aggregate of all those possible values is called a scale. In the case of the operations of the intelligence test, that scale is supposed to represent the concept of IQ. In psychological measurement in general a number of different kinds of measurement are commonly employed: nominal measurement, ratio measurement, ordinal measurement and interval measurement. Psychological testing of intelligence produces an ordinal scale, and the numerical value on this scale is called the intelligence quotient or IQ.

Scaling procedure has its origins in the writings and ideas of the 'operationalists' (for example, Campbell, Bridgeman, Dingle) whilst psychological testing as such has its origins in the work of Galton, Binet, Simon, Wechsler and others and is further elaborated in the work of Vernon. Burt introduced the notion of writing answers in a test booklet, as opposed to the oral question and answer method used by Binet, and Stern suggested the expression of test scores in the form of intelligence quotients.

The epistemological problems deeply embedded in operationalism have long been recognized. David and Judith Willer define operationalism as follows:

*Operationalism* is concerned in general with the formation of empirical categories through experience and in particular with determining systematic operations to be carried out in order to achieve those empirical categories. The basic assumption behind these procedures is that empirical categories can best be defined by the operations used to observe the experiences to be included in the categories. The purpose of operational procedures is to structure these operations so that different results can be assigned numerical values. (Willers, 1973, p. 106.)

As we have already noted, 'scales' are derived from the aggregate of all possible values assigned to results of a succession of similar operations performed on a succession of similar objects. As the Willers point out, the 'scale' is supposed to represent a 'concept'. Thus, 'the concept of I.Q. is what the I.Q. test measures'. The Willers argue that the operationalists have confused concepts with observational categories.[17] Since IQ is defined by the operations of the IQ test, it is not a concept which can enter, for example, into mathematical relations with other concepts, but rather, IQ is an observational category. The Willers go on to argue that,

the 'operation' proposed by the operationalists are simply rules by means of which empiricists can make observations. Operationalism, then, is merely a branch of empiricism which concentrates on the measurement of observational categories. (ibid., p. 107)

IQ scales are measures based on observational categories, that is, on the operations of the IQ test. Psychometric testers and the designers of such tests usually discuss IQ scaling with reference to 'validity' and 'reliability'. The issue of validity is usually couched in terms of questions such as 'How can we know that our IQ measures really measure IQ?'. Psychometrists avoid the attribution of meaning to scores recorded on tests other than that contained in the operationalist definition that 'the concept of IQ is what the IQ test measures'. Thus, a score on an IQ test has meaning only in respect to the test and the operations and measurement of the operations to which that score pertains. Nevertheless, it is evident that scores on IQ tests have had, and indeed still do have, other meaning to those educationalists and administrators who use them. In order to justify definite practices based on IQ test scores, practices which themselves go well beyond anything that could be justifiably based on IQ tests and resultant scores, certain educationalists, administrators and the psychometric testers themselves have sought to establish the 'reliability' and the 'validity' of scaling.

For the operationalists from whom educationalists seek assurances as to the validity of their practices, the question 'How can we know that our IQ measures really measure IQ?' is meaningless. Obviously it measures IQ because 'IQ is what it measures'.

Of course, outside psychometrics there are some well known and influential definitions of intelligence. The authors of these definitions may or may not be involved in psychometrics. The point is that these definitions are extra psychometric definitions of intelligence and/or intellectual activity. For example, 'to judge well, to comprehend well, to reason well, these are the essential activities of intelligence' (Binet and Simon); the ability 'to carry on abstract thinking' (Terman); 'the aggregate or global capacity of the individual to act properly, to think rationally, and to deal effectively with his environment' (Wechsler); 'intelligent activity consists in grasping the essentials in a situation and responding appropriately to them (Heim); and 'innate, general, cognitive ability' (Burt). Now although these definitions emphasize abstract reasoning ability, and in this they share a common characteristic of IQ tests, they do not constitute a coherent conception of intelligence. On the contrary, they constitute no more than a collection of descriptions. In fact despite the prominence of the notion of 'intelligence' in psychology and in educational theories there is no coherent concept of intelligence, let alone a coherent conception of a systematic relationship between it and IQ scores. This is widely acknowledged, and leads to the definition that 'intelligence is what intelligence tests measure'. This however, brings us full circle.

In practice, psychometric testers 'validate' a particular test by correlating scores on the test with some other criterion of the ability or behaviour allegedly assessed by the test. This criterion has to be external to and independent of the items in the test otherwise the procedure is circular. In practice educational success is the most common external criterion used. Unfortunately for the psychometric testers this introduces a circularity at another level. This is because IQ tests are frequently used as important elements of 'scholastic aptitude' tests to determine streaming within many comprehensive schools and as such become the criteria for the allocation of resources (including more able and better qualified teachers) and the placement of pupils. Hence, in practice, the argument that IQ and related tests are effective predictors of future performance is circular. If, however, a procedure is adopted which ensures that future performance is not used as a means of validation this circularity can, of course, be avoided. Nonetheless, the question of the statistical validity, or otherwise, has no necessary relation to criteria of educational validity. The latter can only be judged in terms of the aims and objectives of specific educational policy.

The question of 'reliability' is usually considered to be even more crucial because the reliability of a test must limit its validity. Questions here are usually concerned with whether the same group will score similarly at two different times. A major problem here is that this notion makes the assumption that IQ is an invariant property of individuals (at least over a relatively short period of time). If the assumption is correct and the results are different on the different occasions the psychometric tester would have to conclude that the test was not reliable. On the other hand, if the results were not dissimilar but the psychometric tester assumed 'intelligence' to have 'developmental' characteristics then the test would in this case not be reliable either. Hence, the question of 'reliability' itself depends on conceptions of intelligence and on conceptions of what it is that IQ and IQ tests are measures of. We have seen that there is no coherent conception of intelligence and no coherent conception of a systematic relationship between 'intelligence' and IQ scores.

It is important to repeat, here, that nothing that has been said can be taken to imply that there are no individual human differences. All that we have said is that the psychometric means of measurement of differences in 'intelligence' are limited in a number of ways. Of course, the problems surrounding the notion of 'intelligence' and IQ testing have been identified by many psychologists who reject the pretensions of psychometric testing and the limits of certain branches of psychology. This is particularly true of those progressive educational psychologists who recognize the destructive influence of IQ testing and in particular its use in affecting the distribution of educational resources. Two distinct positions are to be found amongst such educational psychologists. There are those who take a 'sociologistic' view of IQ test results and others who reject the whole notion of the validity of IQ testing for reasons similar to those delineated above.

Now the Bowles, Gintis and Meyer critique of IQism involves statistical methods in which numerical values for IQ and for other factors are variously 'held constant' and the numerical values for IQ enter into arithmetical relations with numerical values attached to other factors. This technique allows them to 'demonstrate the truth' of their proposition that 'the intergenerational transmission of social and economic status operates primarily via non-cognitive mechanisms'. I am not arguing against Bowles, Gintis and Meyer that this proposition is 'untrue' but rather that it cannot be substantiated by the means which they adopt. Their account supposes that IQ scales are a measure of 'cognitive' ability and that the latter can enter into arithmetical relations with numerical values attached to other factors (in this case social and economic status).

However, there are no means by which systematic relations can be established between IQ scales and supposed numerical scales which pertain to 'cognitive ability'. In fact, IQ tests cannot and do not measure only cognitive ability. This is not simply because the latter cannot be studied or measured in isolation from social and motivational determinants, but because the notion of its existence in isolation from social and motivational determinants does not make sense. The IQ scales are not measures of cognitive ability because what they measure is IQ. Furthermore, the IQ scale is an ordinal scale and not a concept which can enter into arithmetical relations with other concepts.[18] As such it can no more be used to 'prove' a negative case than it can a positive case.

To conclude, despite their virulent attack on 'IQism' Bowles, Gintis and Meyer, like many other critics, implicitly accept the validity of psychometric tests in order to attempt to 'prove' their negative case. That is, in attempting to prove that IQism is an incorrect theory of social and economic inequality and that such inequality is not a function of 'environmental' and/or 'genetic' IQ, Bowles, Gintis and Meyer implicitly accept that IQ scales are indeed measures of cognitive ability. Furthermore, the 'legitimation function' that IQism is supposed to perform is never substantiated. That is to say, Bowles, Gintis and Meyer do not demonstrate that *any* of the 'major aspects of the educational process', of which IQism is highlighted as significant, perform a legitimation function. In fact, despite the constant reference to legitimation this concept is never systematically developed beyond the level of rhetoric.

## (iv)  EDUCATION AND SOCIALIST TRANSFORMATION IN BOWLES AND GINTIS' WORK

Bowles and Gintis argue that in capitalist societies schooling has the effect of 'distorting' 'human nature' and in particular it functions to alienate human individuals from their 'true consciousness'. Education functions to reproduce the forms of consciousness required by the capitalist class and the production processes that they have instituted and which they control. The forms of organization of the work processes in capitalist society involve 'hierarchical control' and the interpersonal relations which such control involves are referred to as 'relations of production'. The schooling system in capitalist societies 'mirrors' the forms of organization of work processes and thus reflects their 'needs'. Bowles and Gintis are concerned with the transformation of capitalist society and the transition to socialism. This transformation is the concern of the final chapter of *Schooling in Capitalist America*. We shall examine their argument.

Bowles and Gintis argue that, 'education need distort human development only to the extent demanded by the repressiveness of the social relationships of adult life' (p. 274). The social relationships of adult life to which Bowles and Gintis refer are primarily those of the work process and they argue that the characteristics of the education system 'flow directly from its role in producing a work force able and willing to staff occupational positions in the capitalist system' (p. 255). These occupational positions are 'hierarchical'. Revolutionary change which Bowles and Gintis regard as 'necessary' involves fundamental changes in the economy and in the work processes in the economy. Such changes involve the transition from hierarchical to non-hierarchical forms of organization of the work processes which themselves involve forms of interpersonal 'relations of production'. Thus change in the forms of relations of production, for Bowles and Gintis, is reducible to changes from hierarchical to non-hierarchical forms of organization and the changes in interpersonal 'relations of production'. We have already seen, in an earlier chapter, that relations of production cannot be reduced to interpersonal relations because relations of production can involve non-human forms of economic agents such as joint-stock companies, religious orders, etc. Capitalist production does not necessarily involve human forms of capitalists. Hence changes in the forms of organization of the work process (important as these might be) do not necessarily involve the transformation of capitalist economies and the transition to socialist economies. Nevertheless, this is precisely what the 'revolutionary transformation of the economy' is reducible to in Bowles and Gintis' conception of socialist transformation.

Bowles and Gintis argue that educational change and in particular the move to non-hierarchical forms of organization of schooling can only result from changes in the economy. They argue that, 'an equal and liberating educational system can only emerge from a broad-based movement dedicated to the transformation of economic life' (p. 266). They go on to say that in America 'we need, in short, a second American revolution—and a more democratic, egalitarian, and participatory one at that' (p. 282), and they go on to pose the question: 'How do we get there?'. Their immediate answer to their own question is that they 'have no firm, strongly held, overall, and intellectually coherent answer to this central question' (p. 282). We shall see that not only do they have no answer to their own question but their own conception of capitalist society and the function of the educational system in capitalist society renders their conception of transition to socialism impossible.

Bowles and Gintis argue that socialist transformation can only come about through changes in consciousness and the practices in economic life. The education system can only change as a function of the changes in economic life (the processes of production) because it mirrors the forms of organization found in the processes in the economy. The problem is immediately clear. If the education system reproduces the forms of consciousness 'required' by the economy and the education system can only change as an effect of changes in the economy, and in particular in the practices and the interpersonal relationships in the work processes of capitalism which it mirrors, change appears to be impossible.

This problem, which is a problem within their own theoretical discourse, is recognized a dozen pages from the end of *Schooling in Capitalist America*. Their 'solution' to this theoretical problem has the effect of destroying the theoretical basis of their book, which is a critique of schooling in capitalist society. They argue that,

> The work process produces people as well as commodities. But people, unlike commodities, can never be produced exactly to capitalist specifications. The product—including the experienced needs of people—depends both upon the raw material with which the production process begins, and the 'treatment' it receives. Neither is by any means under the full control of the capitalist class. (p. 277)

They go on to argue that 'what is critical here is that people bring to the process of personal development something independent of the wills of the capitalist class' (p. 278).

It would appear that the work process, and the educational process and the system of relations it is alleged to mirror, is subject to a double determination. On the one hand the work process and its mirror image, the educational process, are determined by the capitalist class and at the same time the human individuals involved in the process are conceived as transcending the wills of the capitalist class. However, the whole of Bowles and Gintis' critique of schooling and the economy in capitalist society is based on the notion that the process of work and educational system are determined by, and are structured to meet the needs of, the capitalist class. Bowles and Gintis are able to posit a conception of human personal development and its independent characteristics only at the cost of their theoretical coherence. Their 'strategies for social change' which appear in the last seven pages of *Schooling in Capitalist America* appear as an afterthought. They subvert the theoretical argument which constitutes the rest of the text.

## CONCLUSIONS

In this chapter we have examined Bowles and Gintis' conception of what they call the 'Political Economy' of education in capitalist societies. We have shown that their epistemological critique of Illich's *Deschooling Society* is unable to establish the basis for what they claim is Marxian theory of education, and that they are not able to establish a coherent theory within their own discourse. We have shown that their attempts to establish the relations between the educational system and the economy are theoretically incoherent.

In the foregoing discussion of IQism as an allegedly 'legitimating' ideology, criticism has been levelled at the notion of IQ testing and assumptions concerning the nature of 'intelligence' contained within the notion of IQ. This critique has not involved a contribution to, and should not be seen as a contribution to, the debate concerning the relative importance of genetic vs environmental/cultural determinants of IQ but rather as a critique of the notion of IQ as such. This critique transcends the traditional terms of the debate. Bowles and Gintis ask why it is that the social function of intelligence (the correlation between IQ and economic success) is so 'blandly accepted' by the 'liberal counterattack' to the conservative genetic school. We could ask why the notion of IQ itself is so blandly accepted by Bowles and Gintis?

Bowles and Gintis argue that the issue of whether IQ is heritable or not is of little relevance to an understanding of 'poverty, wealth and inequality of opportunity in the U.S'. These conclusions at which Bowles and Gintis arrive are based on an economistic reductionist conception of capitalist society and relations between the educational system and the economy. Bowles and Gintis argue that the educational system produces skills in great profusion and that there are possibilities for the acquisition of additional skills 'on-the-job'. They argue that the association between education and 'economic success' is not related to the acquisition of cognitive skills. They argue that skill differences amongst individuals are of little economic importance. It is implicit in Bowles and Gintis' argument that educational inequalities and the attempts to reduce them are largely irrelevant. Inequality is an effect of the normal operations of the basic economic institutions of capitalist society and an individual's 'economic position' is largely independent of 'intellectual success'. Economic inequalities determine educational inequalities and the attempt to reduce educational inequalities as such is, therefore, futile. Their conclusion concerning educational inequalities is based on an economistic reductionist and deterministic conception of the relations between the economy and the education system. Economic 'needs' determine the nature of the educational system. It is this argument that is the basis for their argument that the IQ debate is irrelevant to the issue of equality of opportunity. It would not be possible to sustain the argument that in Britain the notion of IQ has been irrelevant in the distribution of educational opportunity and in particular the inequality of educational opportunity. For Bowles and Gintis, however, inequalities of educational opportunity are simply an effect of inequalities in the economy and in its normal operations, and thus have no independent existence.

A non-determinist, non-reductionist conception of relations between education and skill acquisition and the economy can conceive of skills and skill differences as contributing to individual 'economic success' (given the availability of appropriate occupations in the economy) and also of the possibility of inequalities in the opportunities to acquire skills which could command access to 'economically successful' positions in the economy. In this respect the notion that IQ tests are a measure of 'intelligence' and that the latter is largely determined by heredity has been of primary importance not simply in providing 'legitimation' for economic outcomes for individuals but in actually *affecting* them. Selection in education, based on the notion of IQ, has actively contributed to the inequalities in the distribution of educational opportunities. The IQ debate, therefore, has been of fundamental importance to education in that the critique of the notion of IQ and of IQ testing has challenged an educational practice[19] which has, at least in Britain, contributed to inequality in the distribution of educational provision and opportunity. This is not to argue that inequalities in educational opportunity and educational provision is all that presents an obstacle to a more egalitarian society, but that the nature of education and the practices within the educational system are important to a non-reductionist conception of society.

Finally, we have shown that whilst Bowles and Gintis base their critique of the processes of education and work on the notion that the educational system functions to reproduce the forms of consciousness and skills 'required' by the capitalist class and the work processes that they institute and control, their conception of social change and its possibility subverts the theoretical basis of their argument. Social change is possible for Bowles and Gintis only at the cost of the theoretical coherence of the discourse which forms their critique of schooling in capitalist society.

# 6 Conclusion: Education and the Left in Britain

'I served my apprenticeship to the revolution', he said, 'in the struggle against the Reform Bill of 1832.'

'Against it!' I cried.

'Aye, against it', he said. 'Old as I am, my blood still boils when I think of the way in which a capitalist tailor named Place—one of the half-hearted Radical vermin—worked that infamous conspiracy to enfranchise the middle class and deny the vote to working men. I spoke against it on every platform in England. The Duke of Wellington himself said to me that he disapproved of revolutionists in general, but that he wished there were a few more in the country of my kidney. Then came Chartism with its five points to fool the people and keep them from going to the root of the matter by abolishing kings, priests and private property. I shewed up its leaders, and had the satisfaction of seeing them all go to prison and come out without a single follower left to them. Next came those black spots on our Statute Books, the Factory Acts, which recognised and regulated and legalised the accursed exploitation of the wives and children of the poor in the factory hells. Why, when I took the fight against them, the very employers themselves said I was right . . . Then came . . . the Education Act to drive all our children into their prisons of schools, and drill them into submission, and teach them to be more efficient slaves . . . I left the International because it would not support me against the school Bastilles. (Bernard Shaw's Joe Budgett in his *The Death of an old Revolutionary Hero*)[1]

The ghost of Joe Budgett wanders aimlessly through contemporary theories in sociology of education. It haunts the work of Althusser, Bowles and Gintis, Freire, Illich, Keddie, Young and many of their followers. The purpose of this final chapter is to discuss further the consequences of the theories examined for educational provision and for pedagogic practice and to explore the possible arenas of progress and the role of education in the struggle for democratic socialism in Britain today.

In the preceding chapters we have examined some contemporary theories and arguments in the sociology of education and discussed their limitations. We have examined the 'traditional' theories in the sociology of education and have distinguished them from, and made a distinction between, radical and Marxist theories. In the current debates it is clear that radical rather than Marxist theory has had the most active effect amongst those of the Left, and those who see themselves as Left-radicals and Left-libertarians, working in the sphere of education either as teachers or in some other related capacity. Marxist theory of education has, on the contrary, had little effect. A major reason for this is in the level of generality of Marxist theory and the aspects of it that appear relevant to sociology of education. For example, what conclusions is the Althusserian Marxist educationalist to draw from the general theory of ideology presented in the ISA paper even when it includes an account of the educational ISA as the dominant Ideological State Apparatus in mature capitalist social formations? Just as we have seen that Althusser is unable to maintain his general theory of ideology, the Althusserian Marxist educationalist can refer also to exceptions to the general theory. He/she can be one of those of whom Althusser asks pardon:

> I ask the pardon of those teachers who, in dreadful conditions, attempt to turn the few weapons they can find in the history and learning they 'teach' against the ideology, the system and the practices in which they are trapped. They are a kind of hero. (Althusser, 1971, p. 148)

There can be little doubt, on the other hand, that the traditional sociology of education affected educational policy and that in its challenge the new sociology of education sought to affect pedagogic practice. In posing a direct challenge to the sociology of education that developed in the 1950s and 60s, the new sociology of education confronted the well-established achievement of the former. Such achievement went well beyond the level of description in that it successfully influenced educational policy. The stranglehold of psychometric testing as a major instrument in the allocation of educational resources was broken and the distribution of resources themselves was established as a major source of differential educational attainment. This is not to suggest that there are no unresolved theoretical problems or debates within the traditional sociology of education, nor indeed, that there are no other formal and informal means of differential allocation of educational resources. Nevertheless, the considerable influence of that sociology is evident in the Government reports on education and its organization, commissioned in the late 1950s and in the 60s, and in the move towards the reorganization of secondary education on non-selective lines, pursued in particular by socialists within and outside the Labour Party and initiated by the Labour Government's directives to the Local Education Authorities in the 1960s and early 1970s. This is not to suggest, of course, that such a reorganization is complete, even in the formal sense, or that there are no further policy issues to be fought out concerning the character and the objectives of the comprehensive schools themselves.

It is precisely in the area of educational policy and the means of affecting it that a major distinction is to be found between the traditional sociology of education and its radical challenge. In terms of affecting educational policy the new sociology of education makes appeals directly to practising teachers, urging them to take what it calls a radical view of their own pedagogic practice. The latter is alleged to involve the political activity of imposing meanings, as we have already seen. Conversely, the traditional sociology of education in Britain considered that the major problems for analysis and for changes in policy concerned the distribution of resources and the social class differentials in educational achievement. In its concern with these issues much of the research findings implied that any solutions to what it considered to be the main problems lay largely outside, and were not reducible to, the immediate sphere of teachers' everyday practice. They were problems that could only be seriously tackled by large-scale intervention in the process of distribution of educational resources and in the improvement of housing, health and other spheres of social life.[2] Given the complex nature of control over education, any intervention would involve political initiative and the struggle for policy changes at both central and local government levels. The work of the traditional sociologists of education, and in particular their exposition of the inequalities in educational opportunity and achievement, provided much of the argument for the reform of educational provision in the parliamentary struggle and the struggle at the level of local government. On the other hand,

'new direction' sociology of education has tended to focus . . . upon the ways in which teachers and pupils make sense of their everyday experiences, and on how educational 'reality' is continuously recon-structed in the interaction of individuals, rather than imposed upon them by mysterious external forces. Linked to this change of emphasis has been a refusal to regard definitions of what counts as 'education' as somehow neutral and irrelevant to the way in which inequality is produced in school and society. From such a perspective, what secretly keeps society going is crucially the practices of individual teachers and pupils, and the assumptions about knowledge, ability, teaching, and learning, which are embedded in them. (Whitty and Young, 1976, p. 2)

Whitty and Young thus describe aspects of Young's work, and here as in their more recent book *Society, State and Schooling* a partially critical view of the new sociology of education is adopted. This criticism, such as it is, fails to subvert the theoretical basis of the new sociology of education. Their 'critique' is at an altogether different level.

One of the problems that Whitty and Young detect in the new sociology is that,

> The implication that an invitation to teachers to suspend their taken-for-granted assumptions and to examine critically their own practices would produce a transformation in the nature of their activities was ludicrously naive. (Whitty and Young, 1976, p. 2)

Now, it is not at all ludicrously naïve to assume that workers (in this case teachers) might change their practices as a result of critically examining them. Whilst it is not possible to assess the precise effects of Young's contribution to the sociology of education through his papers in *Knowledge and Control* and through his later publications, it is clear that his writings are available to a large audience, and in particular to an audience of education-alists.[3] It is clear from Young's writings and from the recent disclaimers that the radicals conceived of the mode of affecting educational systems as a process of affecting practising teachers and their 'consciousness'.

## A. RADICALISM, EDUCATIONAL POLICY AND SCHOOLING

In their recent book *Society, State and Schooling*, Young and Whitty, who tell us that they are socialists working within education, suggest that 'many of those who consider themselves to be on the Left in politics have begun to take seriously . . . the suggestion that compulsory schooling for all may be counter-productive for the realization of their political ideals'. One of the problems with the New Directions and its subsequent developments and 're-conceptualizations' is that it has failed to tackle many of the issues that the traditional sociology of education had posed and therefore its so-called 'redefining' of problems involves much evasion. For example, despite its references to 'politics', as we have seen in chapter 2 the determination of the political character of education, one of the chosen realms of the new sociology, is impossible within Young's sociological project. The question of 'political ideals' is a different question to that of the alleged political character of education, but here again there is little more than vacuous rhetoric.

A brief comment is necessary here on the distinction between education and schooling because the antagonism of many of the radicals is towards 'schooling'. Writers such as Illich, Reimer, Freire, Young and Whitty and many others make much of the distinction. It is at the basis of Illich's *Deschooling Society* for example, and in their book *Society, State and Schooling* Young and Whitty insist that

> For many years the reformist wing of British politics, whether liberal, socialist or even Marxist in inclination, has tended to blur any distinctions between education and schooling, and treat the extension of compulsory state education as unambiguously offering the potential for a just society. (p. 1)

They go on to argue that the 'prevailing faith in the school system' amongst radicals derives from a 'failure to analyse critically the concepts of "education" and "society" with which they are operating'. Their argument here and in the work of Illich and others is that schooling should not be confused with education, and it is implied that the radical antagonism is not towards education but towards 'schooling'. The two are not to be confused and conflated because education is a 'good thing' whilst schooling, which goes on in contemporary educational systems, should not be assumed to be a 'good thing'.[4]

There is, of course, an important issue here, for it is clear that there are many important and difficult problems which face teachers, their pupils and students, and educationalists generally, and many cases where 'education' is not achieved. However, the insistence on this distinction will not, on its own, solve any of these problems. Whilst it is recognized that there are many problems within contemporary educational systems, it is argued here that such a distinction is itself fraught with problems.

The distinction between education and schooling involves a contraposition of the form of training that children in contemporary schools undergo, with a utopian ideal of what education 'should be'. Teachers and educationalists generally must, of course, aim for effective *education*. Nevertheless, in positing some utopian ideal the radicals open contemporary educational systems to the continual charge that they are 'schooling' rather than 'educating', because of the failure to meet some ideal criteria. Criteria which are, furthermore, never specified by the radicals who are reluctant to set out their educational policy and aims. Contemporary educational systems are set the impossible task of achieving *unspecified*, utopian, aims lest they be designated 'schooling' systems by their critics. I am not arguing that there are no problems in contemporary educational systems, but rather that such problems that exist should be identified and tackled. The radical sociologists who merely denigrate contemporary educational systems *avoid* such issues. What is more, the alternatives they 'point to' and the pedagogic practices they would implement involve an antagonism to the education of schoolchildren in the name of an antagonism towards schooling. Rather than seeking the improvement of contemporary systems and a move to- wards what they call 'real' education (Illich) they rule themselves out of the political struggles for the effective implementation of educational policy through their denigration of schooling. Their antagonism towards school- ing leads the radical sociologists towards the utopian politics of the deschoolers. The writings of the radicals, unlike those of the traditional sociology of education, have been ignored by central and local government because they provide no grounds for policy and no appeal to any political party of significance. Indeed, the hostility of the radicals to political parties is striking. Illich has remarked that the deschooling movement is a programme without a party; the British radicals likewise are isolated from, and their ideology ignored by, significant political parties. Their mode of affecting educational systems is through affecting the pedagogic practice of teachers by changing their consciousness. We have suggested that the major problem with the radical notion of the means of affecting educational change is not its naïvety but its vacuousness; its failure to provide serious leadership in the form of progressive ideas. It provides empty slogans rather than serious analysis and ideas as the basis for policy.

## (i) THE RADICALS AND TEACHERS

We have seen that whilst the traditional sociology of education had considerable political influence at governmental level, the new sociology aimed to change the consciousness of teachers. Now, only a reductionist conception of politics, that is a conception of governmental politics as the only and the essential level at which effects might be felt, could dismiss this as a serious arena of struggle. The issue here is not that the attempt to change teachers' ideology is naïve or insignificant. The issue is precisely the nature of this change in consciousness or ideology; its content. We have already shown that the radical attack on the politics of educational knowledge cannot be sustained and that much of the radical sociology of education is at best empty rhetoric and at worst leads to an antagonism to education.

In their recent books Young and Whitty retain the general aim of affecting those in training. Their editorial conclusion to *Explorations in the Politics of School Knowledge* is that,

> We trust . . . that these papers will not be treated merely as a body of knowledge to be learned for a degree or a diploma but hope that they will be seen instead as a meaningful contribution to efforts being made in a whole variety of contexts to create a socialist future. (p. 5)

Those readers who venture into the pages of *Explorations* will no doubt reach their own conclusions on the significance of its contribution. As books aimed at those in training both *Explorations* and *Society, State and Schooling* are unsuccessful. Both presuppose a reading of the previous polemical debates initiated by the radicals in the sociology of education. Even Young and Whitty agree that much of the argument put forward by the new sociology of education was confused.

This problem is compounded by the inconsistency between Whitty and Young's editorial commentary and the articles which appear in the books. It is not that such consistency is an essential ingredient to their project, but rather that the absence of discussion of differences leaves the reader, and particularly the reader at which they are aiming, at something of a loss. For example, in Whitty and Young's editorial commentary on the final section of *Society, State and Schooling* titled 'Beyond Critiques' we are told that in a paper in this section Frith and Corrigan,[5]

> locate the politics of education firmly in the wider politics of the struggle for socialism. Much of their paper is concerned with the pervasive state of confusion and contradiction in the educational theory and practice of the Left. (p. 229)

Now, it is far from clear that this paper dispels the confusion but Frith and Corrigan, nevertheless, have an advantage over their editors in that they at least give some indication of what they mean by politics. They insist on political struggle through existing political parties and on discussion of socialist strategy and educational policy.

In their insistence on distinguishing between political parties and their policies for education in contemporary Britain, Frith and Corrigan distinguish between what they call the 'moderate Tory tradition of education, symbolised by Sir Edward Boyle' and that which has replaced it, which they refer to as 'the new spokesmen, Norman St John Stevas and Rhodes Boyson [who] provide political muscle and legitimation for an aggressive Right wing educational ideology'. Frith and Corrigan add that the Left should not underestimate the Right's power' and give the example of the rise to respectability (amongst Tories) of the voucher scheme. On the other hand, in their postscript just fifteen pages later Young and Whitty argue that,

> when leading Labour Party politicians do attempt to intervene directly in what have conventionally been regarded as 'professional matters' (i.e. educational matters) their views seem barely distinguishable from those of the Conservative Right (Young and Whitty, 1977, p. 269)

Despite the political confusion in Whitty and Young's writings they 'hope that a more adequate analysis of the relations between society, state and schooling will emerge' and that 'socialists working in education and elsewhere will begin to develop more realistic strategies for change'. It would seem, then, that they concede that the work has still to be done despite the not inconsiderable bulk of their own writings. My own conclusion is that like Joe Budgett many of the writers in the sociology of education in recent years represent an obstacle to the advance of educational policies for democratic socialism. The so-called William Tyndale 'affair' provides an excellent illustration.

## (ii)  TYNDALE AND THE LEFT

It is evident that many teachers in Britain are suspicious of what they call encroachment of politics into education. This suspicion is not an exclusive preserve of the Left in education. Many teachers express a fear of the role of education in some supposed future authoritarian state. For the Left there is the spectre of neo-fascism or at least the extreme Right wing of the Tory Party. For others there is the spectre of an authoritarian-style Communism. This fear of political encroachment is interwoven with a 'professionalist' ideology. The upshot is an opposition to 'any attempt to centralise control of the curriculum and take away the responsibility from the professionally trained teachers',[6] and the argument that 'Any control of the curriculum means, inescapably, control of the teaching profession by someone outside the school.'[7]

The merits of such arguments have to be viewed in the context of recent moves towards the democratization of education proposed, for example, in the *Taylor Report*,[8] and in the Green Paper *Education in School: A Consultative Document* (Cmnd. 6869), and indeed, the merits of Taylor and the Green Paper have to be assessed.

The starting point for recent moves towards the democratization of education was the events surrounding the William Tyndale Junior and Infants Schools in Islington, North London between 1973 and 1975. Subsequently, the Auld Report[9] on these events and the Taylor Report which draws on the former and the Green Paper have opened the issue to debate. The central issues are those of 'educational standards', 'control of education' and 'accountability'.

For Whitty and Young and others the William Tyndale affair is instructive for socialists working in education in as much as it has, together with 'the Tameside Judgement, the education cuts and the government's attempts to control assessment and curriculum content',

> served to hasten the end of the deeply-embedded notion that education can be kept out of politics and politics kept out of education . . . [and] highlighted the inescapably political nature of educational practice. (Young and Whitty, 1977, p. 271)

They argue in their introduction to *Explorations in the Politics of School Knowledge*, that the lesson to be learned is that,

> As long as radical teachers remain isolated within their schools, and fail to develop links of solidarity with other teachers or work out ways of concretely identifying themselves with the broader working class movement for the transformation of society, they will lack the support and understanding of those groups upon whose power their capacity to resist the establishment will ultimately depend. (p. 5)

Whitty and Young fail to point out that most of those who put pressure on the ILEA to intervene in the affairs of the William Tyndale school were associated with the broader working class movement[10] and especially the main party of the working class movement, the Labour Party. Their concern was with educational standards of the school. That their concern was valid is borne out by the Auld Report.

It is clear there is a world of difference between the radical Left's conception of education policy and that of the Labour Party. The fact that both refer to their own policy as socialist means, merely, that both have to be analysed and assessed. We have already seen that the radical attack on the politics of educational knowledge leads to an antagonism to contemporary education, to deschooling or to political isolation. We have seen that the arguments put forward by the radicals are at best empty slogans, rhetoric; at worst they lead to the deprivation of children of their formal education. It is little wonder that the radical pedagogy is isolated from wide support. The socialism of Michael F. D. Young is little more than the radicalism of his earlier work. The mask of the new labels to be found in the pages of *Society State and Schooling* and *Explorations in the Politics of School Knowledge* cannot obscure the largely cosmetic change.


## B. EDUCATION AND DEMOCRATIC SOCIALISM

The rejection of the empty slogans and rhetoric of the radicals in education does not necessarily entail rejection of the aims of the socialist movement. To reject the call for the 'creation of a socialist future'[11] as an empty slogan is a starting point for the serious task of developing socialist objectives. Indeed, a major task of the movement for the development of socialist objectives, in educational and other cultural spheres and in economic and political spheres, is the exposure of the nature and the consequences of empty sloganizing and to counter its effects. We have already seen that the radical attack on the politics of educational knowledge cannot be sustained and that rather than promoting conditions for the development of democratic socialism it presents an obstacle to that development.

A socialist society which is democratic presupposes the ability of its people to engage in political debate and in political decision making and calculation. In literate societies much of the background to such calculation and decision making appears in the written form, as well as in other forms. The same is true of the political programmes of parties. Whilst it is true that the media, and in particular television and radio, play a significant role in the dissemination of political ideas and the background to calculation, its scope is severely limited. Leaving aside the question of the possibility of future or current editorial political bias in the media (which those who fear authoritarianism should not and do not) the very nature of popular media makes the fullest exposition impossible. For example, there has never been a *full* exposition of a programme of a political party in the media for the simple reason that there is never sufficient time or space.

Now, literacy and numeracy alone guarantees neither that the mass of the people will become involved in informed political debate, nor that they will support socialist policies. The latter is a *political* task for socialists. The general cultural and political education of the mass of the population does not guarantee anything. But the deprivation of the people of the widest access to the forms of discourse in which policy debates are conducted does guarantee their exclusion from informed political debate and presents an obstacle to the development of democracy and therefore an obstacle to the development of democratic socialism. The struggle for democracy and the struggle for democratic socialism involve the reform of social, political and economic institutions. The struggle for educational reform is important in two ways. Firstly, it is an end in itself because the struggle for socialism is the struggle for democratic access to institutions of which education is one. Secondly, educational reform is important in the development of the conditions of existence of democracy in other institutions. For example, workers' control presupposes the ability of a wide range of workers to engage in informed democratic decision making and calculation.[12]

For the ultra-Left, of course, socialism cannot be won by reforms. The slogan 'revolution' is opposed to 'reformism'.[13] The slogan 'revolution' used by the ultra-Left masks the baldness of their analysis and usually means 'insurrection'.[14] They argue that no socialism can be won without insurrection and by that they usually mean a re-enactment of the Bolshevik seizure of power in 1917. Such an ideology not only ignores the difference between Britain in the 1980s and Russia in 1917, it also appears as a substitute for serious political work and amounts to political abstentionism.[15]

We can now bring together a number of issues which have only been hinted at so far but which are nevertheless of importance to socialists. Let us begin with the issue of the role of education in socialist construction and the issue of socialist construction as such. The questions which are usually posed here are what are the political objectives of socialism and what role might education play in democratic socialist society? Now, the radical sociologists who pose these questions usually answer them with somewhat vague answers which include the notion of 'equality', and the role of education is to foster that equality. The precise nature of equality might range from political to social and economic equality and beyond these general phrases it is usually asserted, for example, that 'education will be different under socialism'.

There are a number of related problems with these formulations. A primary problem is the general issue of the objectives of socialism which includes the notional objective of equality. A related problem with reference to education is that of the function of education in providing equality. However, the major problem is in the terms in which the question of socialism and education is posed and *the way it is answered*. The question of what role education will play in a socialist society is only slightly less ridiculous than the answer that education will be different under socialism. The reason why this question and the answer are ridiculous is not because they are not laudable but because they are vacuous. Moreover, they avoid posing the logically prior, and politically more significant question, of the means of achieving socialist objectives and the role of education in contributing towards those objectives. Questions about the role of education in socialism invariably lead to utopian speculation, as indeed they must if the question of the means of achievement of democratic socialism is not posed first.

Once the question of the role of institutions such as education in the transition to socialism is posed as a serious question, rather than easy answers emerging there emerges a whole range of political problems; problems which are masked by simplistic 'revolutionist' slogans. Firstly, it becomes clear that institutions do not transform themselves as an effect of changes in the economic base but rather, definite policies are necessary. These policies must take the prevailing political, cultural-ideological, social and economic circumstances seriously. They are the starting point for socialist (or indeed any other) politics. To put off regarding them as such is to leave politics to the political opponents of socialism. Once this is accepted by socialists the ridiculous notion of having first to wait for the revolution or at least a 'revolutionary situation' or 'era' before engaging in serious policy initiatives towards the instititions can be set aside and work can begin. At the beginning it will be found that others calling themselves by all kinds of names already occupy the field and occupy levels of differing strategic importance. The anti-democratic and bureaucratized character of that occupation will be enough to drive many socialists back to sloganizing, but that would be merely to avoid politics whilst appearing to engage in politics. It would be self-deception.

If much of the control of institutions is anti-democratic then one of the objectives of socialists will be the political struggle for democracy. Of course, this democracy will not of necessity be socialist democracy—the struggle for socialism is not reducible to the struggle for democracy. The struggle for democracy means a struggle for a hearing for socialist ideas and policies, but these ideas and policies must themselves be developed in the context of current conditions. The struggle for equality of educational opportunity, for example, presupposes analysis of inequality and relations between educational opportunity and other aspects of social life. Educational policy is an important aspect of social policy and any serious attack on inequality of opportunity would involve policies across a broad range of areas including health, education, housing, child care, employment, incomes, taxation, benefits, social welfare, etc. The mechanisms of policy implementation and the politics of such an attack are crucial.

The struggle for equality of opportunity in education is a struggle in which many educationalists who are not socialists are already engaged. It is a struggle for the limitation of the intervention of certain factors in the process of distribution of educational resources. It is quite different from the notion of a struggle for 'equality'. It is important to recognize the possibilities and limits of education in the struggle for socialist objectives. For example, education alone cannot reduce economic inequality because the provision of education and of more equal educational opportunity does not lead to the disappearance of, say, unemployment or low-paid occupations in the economy.[16] Whilst education has a role to play in the struggle for socialist objectives, that role should neither be overestimated nor underestimated. The struggle for equality of educational opportunity is no substitute for struggle in other institutions and spheres of life. Education has a role to play but it can provide no simple magic solutions.

If the question of socialist policy for education cannot be reduced to simplistic slogans about equality, what then might the construction of socialist policy for education involve?[17] We have already said that the struggle for democracy is part of the socialist struggle both as an end in itself (democratic socialism) and as a means for the debate of socialist policy and ideas and their implementation. This struggle necessitates taking the anti-democratic nature of contemporary institutions as a serious political issue and a serious object of political struggle. But it also necessitates the analysis of other aspects of institutions and the construction of policy and ideas. Just as socialist ideas and policy are useless without the struggle for the democratic means of their debate and implementation, democracy cannot facilitate socialist construction if there is no socialist analysis and policy.

Let us take education as our object of democratic and socialist struggle. We need an analysis of its mechanisms and an analysis of the degree of democratization already existing. In the preceding chapters we have examined the state of theory on the Left and discussed its limitations. It is evident that there is no coherent theory of education which can be taken *en bloc* and converted into socialist educational policy. However, we have a number of indications of what social functions and effects education has. The major problem is that they usually appear under the auspices of some 'general theory'. The first step is to reject this general theory but to retain the useful indications that are contained within it. For example, we have rejected Young's general theory that education is necessarily the imposition of meanings of a political character and Althusser's general theory of ideology. Nevertheless, it is clear that specific curricula must be debated by socialists and their limitations exposed and combated. Sexism and racism in the literature used in children's education is an obvious example. Work is already going on in this sphere and by no means exclusively by socialists.

The work of the traditional sociolgists must also be stripped of its generalist character. The class differentials in educational opportunity and achievement in Britain has been well documented.[18] However, the differentials in educational opportunity and achievement are not exclusively of a class character. There are, for example, sexual and regional differences in educational provision and in achievement. The complex nature of educational differentials means that no simplistic sloganizing about education and class is an adequate basis for socialist educational policy. It is not simply the question of the analysis and condemnation of these aspects of education that concerns serious socialists but the means of effecting change. If the issue of class, regional and sexual differences in educational opportunity is coupled with the question of the means of effecting change, then a whole range of political work is opened up. Just as there are regional and individual school differences in educational opportunity, as well as overall class differentials, the nature of educational control in Britain means that there are a range of arenas of political struggle where educational policy is debated and decisions made.

## C. POLITICS AND EDUCATION

There are two main areas of discussion under the heading of 'politics and education'. On the one hand there is the argument surrounding the notion of the supposed dangers of politico-ideological bias creeping into the curriculum. This argument applies across the whole of the curriculum but has particular significance with respect to political education as a subject on the curriculum. The possibility of political bias in the teaching of say, history, is not regarded, as such, as reason for the exclusion of history from the school curriculum. The 'inevitability' of bias in the teaching of politics is used frequently as a reason for its exclusion. In passing it should be noted that the issue of the teaching of the history of say, relations between India and Britain in a society which includes Britons and Indians, poses a real challenge. If educationalists are to avoid the racism of curriculum apartheid they will have to come to terms with, for example, the question as to whether the occupation by the East India Company amounted to systematic economic exploitation or a 'civilizing mission'. Will the answers to such question involve political 'bias'?

On the other hand, arguments under the heading of 'politics and education' are arguments surrounding policy of educational provision and the form of organization of the educational system. Here, discussion is usually in terms of the danger of politically or ideologically doctrinaire policy decisions. Such arguments as whether the Labour Party's scheme for non-selective secondary education is fired by egalitarian ideology or whether the Tory policy for selection was fired by 'élitist' ideology are contraposed to arguments that educational policy should not be a 'political' issue and that the 'interests of the children' or the 'interests of the nation and the economy' should determine educational policy.

Now, both of the areas of discussion of education and politics, that is, the discussion of the political character of the curriculum and the discussion of the political character of policy for provision, share a reductionist conception of politics; politics = ideology or dogma. When it is argued that 'politics should be kept out of education' it is argued that dogma and political ideology should be excluded. The *basis* of these arguments can and has been challenged. Their basis is their reductionist conception of politics.

## (i) POLITICAL EDUCATION AS A SUBJECT ON THE CURRICULUM

It is not necessary to rehearse in full the arguments surrounding the possibility of political education which is not politically biased. Clearly, political education as a subject on the curriculum *can* be subject to political bias, as can other subjects. The *possibility* of bias does not mean that political education *has* to be biased, any more than the possibility of bias in the teaching of history means that history has to be biased. Furthermore, the arguments *for* political education are not confined to any one political theory. For example, Aristotle, J. S. Mill and Karl Marx argue for political education from quite distinct and opposed political theories.[19] On the other hand, argument against political education, as much as argument for political education, depends upon a particular concept of politics or political theory. There is no opposition to, or argument for, political education which does not involve a political stance. In the pages of this book political education is argued for from the political position which seeks the widening of democracy and the politics of democratic socialism. Opposition to political education must involve anti-democratic ideology. It seeks to deprive the population of knowledge of political structure and policy and thus represents an obstacle to informed democratic political debate. The struggle for democracy is the struggle against the political bias of arbitrary exclusion of any policy from democratic debate. The admittance of any policy to the arena of political debate means that the political task of democratic socialists, who are opposed to fascism and racist ideology for example, is to engage in political opposition; to educate and to expose the character and consequences of such political ideologies. It is not enough to drive racism and fascism off the streets; to drive it underground. The political task for socialists is to combat it politically and ideologically in *all* forms and in *all* the places where it appears. In recent times it has appeared in the schools. The National Front attempt to win over schoolchildren is not the reason why political education in schools is necessary; it is a symptom of that necessity.

Now, in many of the discussions for and against political education as a subject on the curriculum, politics is reduced to party politics and/or political ideologies. The dangers are seen as the possibility of bias towards the politics of the Conservative Party or the Labour Party, or towards communist ideology or fascist ideology etc. Political education in a non-reductionist conception, however, would include debate over party policy and ideologies as well as education in the nature of political structure and the arenas of political debate. If politics is conceived in the widest, non-reductionist sense, it is clear that political education would include education in the structure of local as well as national decision making in areas such as housing, social policy, work and employment etc. If politics is conceived as including the making of decisions on the basis of informed democratic debate in a wide range of spheres of social, economic and political life and institutions, including those at national and party level, it follows that political education as a subject on the curriculum is neither reducible to party politics nor to ideological bias. Such a programme presupposes the training of teachers of political education. A serious policy for such training and the widespread inclusion of political education on the school curriculum could be a major force in the struggle for wider democracy and democratic politics in Britain. That struggle cannot be left to democratic forces in education. Education has a role to play in the struggle for democracy but it is not the only sphere in which the struggle can and is being advanced. The significance of education should not be overestimated, but its possibilities should be explored. Education and democratic debate have an important role to play in the struggle against ignorance and predudice and the ideologies which are based on ignorance and prejudice. Arguments which seek to exclude political education from the curriculum actually subvert the democracy they claim to seek to defend and protect.

## (ii)  THE POLITICS OF EDUCATIONAL PROVISION

The second sense in which education and politics is discussed is in terms of the politics of educational provision. At one level there are arguments as to whether the provision (and particularly the reorganization of educational provision along comprehensive lines) of education is an area for party political or ideological struggle and it is sometimes asserted that the 'national interest' or the 'interests of the children' must come first. The political parties reply that their policy for education does seek to promote the national interest and the interests of the children. A second set of arguments is concerned with the division of responsibility for educational provision. Some teachers, for example, argue that responsibility for material provision is the concern of the government and its agencies, whilst responsibility for the curriculum is the concern of 'professionally trained teachers'.[20] In both of these sets of arguments it is alleged that there is a danger of politico-ideological intervention in education, and it is argued that education must not become a 'political tool' of a particular party or ideology. Of course, educational policy is part of social policy, and as such different parties have a legitimate concern and adopt a different policy. The major concern of the opponents to intervention is to resist developments which may lead to education becoming a politico-ideological tool.

Whether or not such fears are well founded, it is clear that all of these arguments are derived from a reductionist conception of politics; politics is reduced to party and ideology. Such a reduction suppresses consideration of important levels of policy calculation and decision making and obscures the possibility of the development of arenas of political debate which themselves could act as forces against authoritarian politics.

Party politics and ideology play a part in the determination of the character of educational provision but it can hardly be reduced to party and party political ideology. The character of educational provision in Britain has a complexity beyond differentials in opportunity in terms of the classes which politics and ideology are supposed to represent. There are sexual differences in opportunity and achievement in education and there are geographical differences. The latter are not simply differences between counties in different parts of the country. Differences occur between different areas within towns. The patterns of educational opportunity in Britain are a complex combination of class, sexual and geographical differences.

Educational policy in Britain is subject to political debate (that is to say debate over policy in a non-reductionist sense) and political influence at a number of levels. None of these levels can be ignored because it is at these levels that the inequalities of educational opportunity are administered. To be aware of the overall patterns of educational inequalities but to ignore the mechanisms of their administration is to neglect possibilities for struggle for change.[21]

Within the class, sexual and geographical differences in educational provision there is complex and uneven provision for individual children. It may be that educational provision for a middle class girl in a particular geographical area may be inferior to that of, say, a lower middle class boy in another geographical area, etc. The precise character of provision cannot be given prior to specific investigation. The investigation of the specific character of educational provision *for individuals* is not the object of sociological investigation. What is important to note is that for an individual, educational provision is subject to a series of levels of determination. Decisions are made at a number of levels and they are subject to various degrees of democratic debate; at some levels there is virtually no democratic debate whatever. A political object for democratic socialists and for other democrats is the opening of these levels to democratic debate; to make the levels or agencies of direction of policy subject to democratic debate.

We have said that to reduce the politics of education to the political struggle at government level between parties in parliament is to ignore other levels of political struggle. This is not to argue that the parliamentary struggle is not significant. Indeed, in recent years this struggle has been highly significant.[22] Nevertheless, central government and its agency the DES is only one of a number of agencies of direction which are of significance in the determination of educational policy. We shall use the term 'agency of direction' to denote agencies which take very different forms. The provision of education for an individual is subject to determination by a complex combination of the following agencies of direction: political parties working through central and local government agencies; arenas of debate at national level (i.e. parliamentary debate and decision) and arenas of debate at local government level; agencies of central and local government such as the DES and the LEAs; individual school heads as agencies of direction; individual teachers; the influences of policy debates and decisions made by teachers' unions and headteachers' unions. There is no particular significance to the order in which these are listed and there may well be others which have been omitted. In some cases there are active parent—teacher associations which may influence policy whilst in other cases there are no parent—teacher associations or they are merely fund-raising bodies. The role of school governors and school governing bodies will be discussed in a moment.

There can be no general theory of the relative influence and significance of the different agencies of direction. The history of comprehensive reorganization has demonstrated this dramatically. National decisions can be frustrated by local authorities. Furthermore, even where central and local governments are at one, policy can be frustrated at the level of the individual school. For example, headteachers so inclined are capable of formally accepting policy decisions of both central and local government whilst surreptitiously adopting practices which effectively nullify that policy. Individual class teachers too can frustrate policy decisions made at other levels by the practices they adopt. Of course, the opposite is also possible and individual teachers and/or headteachers may adopt pedagogic practices which are contrary to those recommended by other agencies of direction. The Tyndale affair is a case in point.

We have already seen that the radical sociologists of education placed most emphasis on the changing of the attitudes of teachers towards their own activity and their pupils. On the other hand, the traditional sociologists of education placed the emphasis on affecting policy at the level of central and local government through the agency of the Labour Party; though not exclusively so. However, once the question of the politics of educational provision is posed in terms of class, sexual and geographical differences and the complex combination of these factors recognized as having different outcomes in different places at different times, the notion of an *essential* level of political struggle must be rejected (as reductionist). It is neither sufficient to indicate the nature of inequality of educational opportunity to agencies of direction in the form of central or local government nor to persuade agencies of direction in the form of individual teachers to change their attitudes. The case of the reorganization of schooling along comprehensive lines again serves as an illustration. Not only is political struggle necessary at both local and central government levels, struggle is also important at the level of the individual school in order to secure effective implementation of policy. The implementation of policy for the comprehensive reorganization of schooling can be frustrated by ideologically unsympathetic heads and teachers. The struggle for the implementation of policy for comprehensive schooling is more than the struggle to repaint the sign on the school gate.

Many socialists as well as non-socialists are concerned and opposed to the lack of open debate at certain levels or arenas of political decision making. The office of headteacher is a particular agency of direction which is not at present open to democratic debate. There are of course many headteachers who run democratic offices and make decisions on the basis of debate with teachers, governors, parents, and the officers of the local education authorities. Nevertheless, the case of William Tyndale again illustrates that the headteacher, as an agency of direction, can function without recourse to democratic debate and democratic decision making for a considerable length of time. The recommendations of the Taylor Report include attempts to democratize the office of headteacher through a restructuring and democratization of the governing bodies of schools.

## (iii) THE TAYLOR REPORT

The recommendations of the Taylor Committee, in *A New Partnership For Our Schools*,[23] include the recommendation that governing bodies of

TABLE 6.1  *Illustration of the proportional division of places on governing bodies which might apply across a range of primary and secondary schools*

| | School Staff (1) | Parents (2) | Local Education Authority (3) | Local Community (4) | Total |
|---|---|---|---|---|---|
| *Primary* (100 pupils, 6 teachers, 1 full-time and 4 part-time ancillaries) ... | 2 | 2 | 2 | 2 | 8 |
| *Primary* (200 pupils, 9 teachers, 3 full-time and 15 part-time ancillaries) ... | 3 | 3 | 3 | 3 | 12 |
| *Junior (7–11)* (350 pupils, 18 teachers, 2 full-time and 25 part-time ancillaries) ... | 3 | 3 | 3 | 3 | 12 |
| *Middle (9–13)* (600 pupils, 30 teachers, 1 full-time and 40 part-time ancillaries) ... | 4 | 4 | 4 | 4 | 16 |
| *Secondary* (600 pupils, 40 teachers, 2 full-time and 35 part-time ancillaries) ... | 4 | 4 | 4 | 4 | 16 |
| *Secondary* (1,100 pupils, 65 teachers, 5 full-time and 50 part-time ancillaries) ... | 5 | 5 | 5 | 5 | 20 |

| | | | | |
|---|---|---|---|---|
| High (11–16) with Adult Education Centre (1,300 pupils, 70 teachers, 5 full-time and 50 part-time ancillaries. 2300 student enrolments, 125 part-time tutors, 20 part-time ancillaries) ... | 6 | 6 | 6 | 6 | 24 |
| Secondary 1,500 pupils, 90 teachers, 8 full-time and 75 part-time ancillaries) ... | 6 | 6 | 6 | 6 | 24 |
| Secondary (1,900 pupils, 110 teachers, 15 full-time and 95 part-time ancillaries) ... | 6 | 6 | 6 | 6 | 24 |

(1) These figures include the place to be reserved for the headteacher and any places allocated by the local education authority for supporting staff.

(2) Any allocation of places for eligible pupils, within these totals, would be determined by the local education authority.

(3) The individuals filling these places could, at the LEA discretion, include members of other local authorities in the area served by the school.

(4) These places would be filled on the recommendation of the governors appointed to represent the 3 other categories of membership. They could include members of local authorities mentioned in (3) above who did not find representation in the LEA group.

Source: A New Partnership For Our Schools (The Taylor Report), Department of Education and Science and Welsh Office. Annex to chapter 4, page 35. Reproduced with the kind permission of the Controller of Her Majesty's Stationery Office.

schools should be composed of 'equal numbers of local education authority representatives, school staff, parents with, where appropriate, pupils and representatives of the local community' (para. 4.6) and that 'the headteacher of a school should always be a member of its governing body and that he be included *ex officio* in the group of members representing the school staff' (para. 4.16).

The committee of enquiry suggests that the places for the staff group, with the exception of the head of course, should be filled through elections in which teachers and supporting staff would vote separately for those of their own number (para. 4.18). The committee recommend that 'priority in the allocation of places within the school staff group on the governing body should be given to teachers' (para. 4.17). Parent governors would be elected from parents of children currently attending the school (para. 4.20) and elected by the parents of the children attending that school (para. 4.22). The appointment of eligible pupils to the governing body (see paras 4.24 to 4.26) would fall within this latter category (see fig. 6.1, note 2).

Local education authority representatives, the Taylor committee suggests, would be decided by the local education authority (para. 4.10) and the representatives of the local community would be co-opted by the governors representing the three other interest groups (i.e. the parents, the school staff and the local education authority representatives) (para. 4.30). An illustration of the proportional division of places on the governing bodies might apply across a range of primary and secondary schools appears as an annex to chapter 4 of the Taylor report, and as Table 6.1.

The recommendations of the Taylor committee, only a few of which can be discussed here, have met with some opposition from teachers. For some teachers, and particularly headteachers, the recommendations of the Taylor committee represent a threat to their professional status and responsibility. A delegate to the 1978 Annual Conference of the National Union of Teachers, for example, is reported to have argued that it is 'a nonsense to suggest that lay people could be involved' and that it was a 'gross injustice of the Taylor Committee to suggest that governors should not only determine the aims of a school but precisely how these aims should be carried out'.[24]

Teachers traditionally regard the provision of adequate resources for curriculum development and other developments as the responsibility of the DES and the local authorities, whilst control of the curriculum is regarded by them as their professional responsibility. Delegates to the NUT Conference reconfirmed this traditional view. *The Teacher* reported one delegate as arguing that teachers 'are the only group that really knows what irreparable damage could be done in education by ill-informed interventions from people who lack professional expertise' and another that 'only teachers are qualified to judge exactly what is right for that school and only then within their own subject speciality'. The conference is reported to have 'voted heavily against any attempt to centralise control of the curriculum and take away the responsibility from professionally trained teachers'.[25] Teachers see the main threats to their 'professional responsibility' over the curriculum as coming from the Green Paper and from the Taylor Report. Both were commissioned by the Labour Government.

The merits and limitations of the report of the Taylor Committee cannot be examined in detail here.[26] For example, categories and the individuals eligible within the categories represented on the governing bodies of the school is an area for further discussion and for debate. Teachers may well feel that the inclusion of the headteachers within the category of school staff, thus reducing their number by one, an issue worthy of further consideration. For many teachers headteachers are as much 'employers' as colleagues. Equally, parents may feel that the depletion of their numbers by the inclusion of eligible pupils within their category an issue for further consideration. It will be teachers who will play a leading role in whatever debate there is to be over the composition of the governing boards. Indeed, it is clear that the support of teachers and their unions is crucial to the effective implementation of the recommendations of the Taylor Committee.

One of the major merits of the Taylor report is that it raises the issue of the democratization of control of the individual school, however limited that democratization may be. The proposals of the Taylor Committee are an attempt to subject not only the activity of teachers to wider debate, but significantly, they attempt to open the role of headteacher to democratic debate. As we have already mentioned, there are headteachers who already run more or less democratic offices and who are open to the debate of their staff, parents, pupils and others. There are others who do not. The recommendations of the Taylor Committee could lead to the establishment of a significant arena of democratic debate.

One of the main arguments of those teachers who oppose Taylor is that they are the best judges of what children at school should do and should learn. This notion is not only narrow minded, it is also illusory. The curriculum is already subject to 'external controls'. The examination boards, for example, influence the curriculum. There is also an external influence which although not felt directly by teachers, is felt by their pupils when they leave school to seek employment. Knowledge and skills expected and required by employers can be ignored by teachers only to the cost of their pupils. Furthermore, individual teachers are subject to the controls imposed on the curriculum by the headteachers. The recommendations of the Taylor Committee have the effect of proposing the opening of relations between undemocratic headteachers and other teachers to democratic debate.

The notion that the Taylor recommendations would lead to the infiltration of the ideology of business and subordinate education 'to the needs of industry' is a fear held only by the conspiracy theorists. Firstly, it is clear that local businessmen would not be able to secure control over the governing bodies outlined by Taylor. Secondly, it is far from clear what forms of curriculum change such businessmen might seek to secure; given the specialized nature of industrial production processes in advanced capitalist economies which mean that training for industry goes on not in schools but in specialized institutions such as apprentice training schools and 'on-the-job'.[27]

The most that local businessmen might be concerned to secure is competence in basics (the three Rs) in the pupils they recruit. There is nothing to fear here (teachers could effectively block any attempt to narrow the curriculum to only the basics) and much to recommend it, for the school leaver who is able to read, write and comprehend instructions on the operation of machinery will also be able to comprehend the policies of the unions at his place of work and read and comprehend the policies of political parties at both the local and national level. The concern of the Green Paper, *Education in Schools: A Consultative Document* (Cmnd. No. 6869) with standards of literacy and numeracy in schools is in no sense a concern which is dissonant with the struggle for democratic socialism. Of course, teachers are right to ensure that the assessment and monitoring of standards does not lead back to anything remotely resembling the 11 +. They have the power to block any such moves. However, just as there is no necessary connection between democratic socialism and the libertarian-anarchic practices of Tyndale or the theories of Illich and his contemporaries, there is no contradiction between democratic socialism and the core curriculum and the three Rs. Furthermore, there is no contradiction between democratic socialism and the subjection of the practices of teachers to democratic debate and control.

The Taylor Committee recommends that parents, and certain eligible pupils, be represented on the governing bodies of schools. The line taken by some teachers with respect to their 'professional responsibility' suggests that parents should have no right to contribute to debates over the education of their children. Such a position is clearly anti-democratic. An arrangement whereby parents and teachers meet with others to debate the curriculum of the school as well as other important issues is surely an opportunity to open and widen the possibility of democratic control to a major social institution. It opens the opportunity for teachers and parents to have a further channel of communication through which teachers could explain the changes that are happening in our schools and explain why. It gives the parents the opportunity to comprehend better such changes and therefore the opportunity for them to take a positive attitude towards them.

The idea that parents and/or businessmen could take control of the curriculum is ludicrous. The curriculum remains the major concern of teachers but the recommendations of the Taylor Committee open the possibility of wider debate over the individual school and make significant moves towards the democratization of the role of the headteacher. If teachers are concerned about the categories of representation on the governing bodies or the numbers within each of the categories, then there is an issue to debate and to campaign over. A dogmatic opposition to Taylor is nothing but an opposition to steps towards democracy. Rather than opposing democracy teachers could turn their abilities towards problematizing its forms.[28]

There has been a good deal of criticism of the Taylor Report, much of which has been ill-considered or misinformed. The recommendations of the report have been criticized at very different levels. In an interesting critical appraisal which points out some of the limitations and difficulties that the recommendations of the Taylor Report involve, Miriam David (1977) argues that,

> Although the Committee addressed the question of the nature of representative democracy for education, it did so in a limited way. It accepted the framework developed for changes in other aspects of the policy process which . . . have not led to more political participation or representation. The changes have been couched within a particular ideology about control of advanced capitalist society which has been called 'managerialism' or 'corporatism'. It has been argued that none of the policy-making changes achieved within this framework has resulted in a real change in power relationships. (Brown, M. and Baldwin, S. (Eds) *The Year Book of Social Policy 1977*, p. 100)

This theme of the determining ideology of corporate capitalism also appears in the work of the Centre for Contemporary Cultural Studies, Birmingham, in the context of a discussion of the limits of 'social democracy' and its educational policy. Discussing the politics of the 'Great Debate' Finn, Grant and Johnson (1977) conclude that:

> The 'Great Debate' has revealed the *metaphorical character* of education. Education, the universal, unifying experience, has become the vehicle, par

excellence, for the exploration of wider social questions. The relationship of education to the economy, the relationship of the individual's development to the 'national interest', captures other themes which are currently part of the political discourse. The bidding for consent, the forging of a new hegemony on the basis of a corporate capitalism, can be seen through the educational debate. Central to both are themes of discipline, and subordination of the individual to the collective interest. The collective interest is now defined, however, less in Labour's old terms of a 'more equal society', but more in terms of the survival of a capitalist economy. (*Working Papers in Contemporary Cultural Studies, 10*, p. 196)

Part of the challenge for democratic socialism is the development of new themes; of alternative socialist ideology and strategy. But it has to make a start with current conditions and to dismiss the initiatives of the Labour Government's Green Paper and the Taylor Report recommendations as merely the effects of 'corporate capitalist ideology' is to drive the Left back into the politico-ideological ghetto.

It must be said that the implementation of the recommendations of the Taylor committee could not be achieved overnight. There are two issues here. Firstly, there is the question of statutory implementation of the recommendations. This question presupposes a majority of members of parliament committed to the broadening of democracy. It is not at all clear that in the present circumstances such conditions exist. Secondly, there is the question of the *effective* implementation of the recommendations in the sense of the informed participation of lay persons (e.g. parents). The latter presupposes both the broadening of awareness of the wider population and the specific training of future governors in matters concerning education and curriculum.

To conclude then, the implementation of the recommendations of the Taylor committee should be seen as a long-term project whose development presupposes certain other developments. The creation of conditions in which democratization might develop is a task for socialists and democrats working within education. A particular struggle of great significance is the struggle within the teaching profession and the teachers' unions to encourage the development of democratic ideology.

Finally, it is worth noting that, contrary to the notions of some teachers, the implementation of the recommendations of the Taylor committee would not mean 'unbridled parental power'. In addition to the reasons already given the governing bodies of individual schools have responsibilities placed upon them by central and local government. In particular, central government and the parliamentary struggle over educational policy would remain a major agent of direction.

## CONCLUSION

I have argued that educational provision is the result of struggles within a numbers of arenas and relations between such arenas. These arenas, or agencies of direction, constitute the mechanisms by which educational policy is formed and through which it is implemented. I have argued that to essentialize any particular arena or agency involves a reductionist conception of politics. To take two instances, government policy and the practices of individual teachers both have their particular significance. The significance of educational policy initiated by Labour Governments in recent years is that it has transformed the educational system in Britain. This transformation has taken the form of the implementation of the comprehensive system. The effective implementation of comprehensive education is a matter in which the parliamentary struggle will continue to play a role. The matter is also the object of policy struggles over the curriculum and the forms of organization of schooling which are resolved at the level of the individual school and the local authorities.

The question of the role of education in social change is a matter of concern to socialists. We have already seen that the commitment of Labour Governments to socialist policies in education is often challenged by the ultra-Left and radical sociologists of education. The Labour Governments' policies towards education and their significance in the struggle for democratic socialism cannot be assumed to be 'given'. They are themselves subject to political debate and political struggle. The nature of this debate and struggle is itself dependent on the nature of the Labour Party and its relations with Labour Governments. To argue that the Labour Party *is* or *is not* a possible vehicle for the development of socialist policies is to assume that the nature of the party and its policies are 'given'. On the contrary, what the party is and what its policies are, as well as its relation to Labour governments, is an object of ongoing political struggle. The role of the Labour Party and Labour Governments in educational policy is a matter of record. Its future role will be determined by struggles over the nature of the Labour Party as such, its relations with Labour Governments, and the educational policy it takes up and develops. These struggles may or may not lead to policy (in education and elsewhere) developments towards democratic socialism.

I have insisted that no particular agency can be regarded as 'essential' in the struggle over educational policy whilst agreeing that certain agencies have had particular strategic importance. An idea which is common amongst the ultra-Left and amongst some radical sociologists is that the educational system can itself bring about the transformation of capitalist economies and the transition to socialist economies by changing the attitudes of future individual workers towards industry and industrial practices and relations. On the other hand it is argued that, 'Through the educational encounter, individuals are induced to accept the degree of powerlessness with which they will be faced as mature workers' (Bowles and Gintis, 1976, p. 265). To change education in such a way as to change these attitudes, it is argued, is to promote the development of socialist economies. A major problem with this argument is that capitalist economies are not reducible to the attitudes of the workers in them. The transformation of capitalist economies involves much more than a change of workers attitudes. It involves the transformation of relations of production which is not reducible to the transformation of interpersonal relations and attitudes. Transformation cannot be reduced to changes of attitudes and interpersonal relations because it involves the transformation of a much wider range of conditions of existence of capitalist relations of production; legal, political, financial etc., as well as cultural (attitudes, values, meanings, etc.).

Education has a role to play in the struggle for democratic socialism and for socialist economies. The education of all classes of people to a level above that required merely to fulfil their economic functions, is a presupposition of the struggle for popular democratic socialism and the transition from capitalist to democratic socialist society. The role of education should neither be under-estimated nor should it be over-estimated. It has a role to play but socialist transformation cannot be reduced to transformation of education and the attitudes of future workers.

Whilst the struggle for wider democratization of social, political and economic institutions presupposes education, it cannot be reduced to the struggle for education and changes of attitude; just as the struggle for socialism cannot be reduced to the struggle for democracy. The struggle for wider education will not guarantee democracy just as the struggle for democracy will not guarantee socialism. Education and informed debate in a democracy merely secure conditions in which socialist and other policies can be debated. Of course, one of the policies of democratic socialism is the development of popular forms of democracy.[29]

The struggle in education is only part of the wider struggle for socialist democracy. For socialists in education the struggle for democratic socialism involves, amongst other things, the struggle for the democratization of the arenas of debate and control of educational policy and practice. These include arenas at central and local levels of government; local government is an arena of struggle that can be ignored only at great cost.[30] It is clear that the struggle for socialism cannot be reduced to the parliamentary struggle or the struggle at the level of local government, despite the crucial significance of both of these levels of debate and control. Important as these struggles are, policy passed at these levels can only be *effectively* implemented, in the case of education, if accepted at the level of the individual school. The implementation of the democratization of the control of the individual school proposed by the recommendations of the Taylor Committee could contribute to the effective implementation of policy and could serve as an important arena of initiation of policy. For the ultra-Left and for the cynical the Taylor Report either does too little or too much. However, in the current situation the implementation of *a programme* of democratization of control of the individual school would be significant in the struggle for democracy and for democratic socialism. The struggle for the implementation of such a programme is a struggle that socialists cannot afford to neglect. The argument put forward by some teachers, that it is the responsibility of local and central government to furnish adequate resources for education and educational developments, whilst responsibility for curriculum is the responsibility of teachers,[31] misses the point that the implementation of the Taylor Report would expand the arena of debate and would link the two areas of responsibility. Both curriculum and the resources necessary to teach it would be subject to debate.

The contribution to innovation in educational policy made by the Labour Party and the Labour Governments of recent years has been significant. The programme of comprehensive reorganization of secondary education and the role of both the Party and Labour Governments in it is of particular significance. More recently, the initiation of debate over the standards achieved in schools by the Green Paper, *Education in Schools: A Consultative Document* (Cmnd. 6869) and the commissioning of the Taylor Report are of particular significance. Now much of the ultra-Leftist literature on politics treats the parliamentary struggle and the Labour Party as arenas of political struggle which are not significant in the struggle for socialism. The ultra-Leftist ideology invites abstentionism from political work and substitutes revolutionary slogans and despises all 'reforms'. The ultra-Left is over-populated with Joe Budgetts. Abstentionism and revolutionary sloganizing is easy; serious political work less so.

We have seen that the Labour Party and recent Labour Governments have made serious contributions to educational policy and political debates over education. I have argued, however, that despite the significance of the parliamentary struggle other levels of political struggle are important in the struggle for democratic socialism in Britain today.

The future of democratic socialism lies not in dogma and the rhetoric of empty slogans but in informed, democratic political debate. The role of education in the struggle for democracy and democratic socialism is to contribute to the development of conditions of existence of informed, democratic political debate.

# Notes

## INTRODUCTION

1. Lenin's *Collected Works*, Vol. 28 and reprinted in Lenin (1975).
2. From his *Report to the All-Russian Congress of Political Education Departments*, 17 October 1921, titled 'The New Economic Policy and the Tasks of the Political Education Departments', reprinted in Lenin's *Collected Works*, Vol. 33 and in Lenin (1975).
3. Ibid.
4. Keddie (1973) especially the Introduction. For a critique of Keddie, see my paper to the 1977 Annual Conference of the British Sociological Association, titled 'Critique of the Sociology of the Politics of Educational Knowledge', part II.
5. For a discussion of the conception of the nature of the objects of discourse in rationalist accounts see Hindess and Hirst (1977) especially chapter 1, 'Discourse and Objects of Discourse'.
6. I discuss some of these problems further in my PhD thesis, *Sociological Theories of Ideology and Education*. For a critique of Althusser's theory of ideology see Hirst (1976) and chapter 3 of the present book.
7. For a critique of the 'phenomenological' sociology of Alfred Schutz and for a discussion of the theoretical relation of Schutz to the work of Max Weber see Hindess (1972 and 1977a).
8. Marx and Engels (1968) *Selected Works in One Volume*, pp. 181–5. Other examples can be found in the work of many Marxist writers who retain, either explicitly or implicitly, an Hegelian philosophy of history. See for example, Lukacs's *History and Class Consciousness* (1971).
9. See for example Lenin's *What is to be Done?* (1902).
10. See Hindess and Hirst (1975) especially pp. 272–8, for a critique of the teleology of Althusser's concept of 'structural causality'.
11. See Althusser (1971) for his elaboration of the notion of the educational ISA. The article 'Ideology and Ideological State Apparatuses' is reprinted in Cosin (1972). For a critique see Hirst (1976a and 1976b).
12. For further discussion of modes of critique of theoretical discourse see Hindess and Hirst (1977), Hindess (1977a) and S. P. Savage (1980) *The Theories of Talcott Parsons: The Social Relations of Action*, especially chapter 1.

## CHAPTER 1

1. Berger and Berger (1976) chapter 4, 'What is an Institution? The Case of Language', for example.
2. See Mead (1934).

3. Louis Althusser's use of Lacan's concept of the 'mirror phase' in his theory of ideology is discussed in chapter 3.
4. See Little and Westergaard (1964) for example.
5. For a discussion of Durkheim's theoretical discourse see Hirst (1975).
6. Ibid.
7. In Parsons (1964). The paper was published originally in the *Harvard Educational Review*, 29:4 (1959) and has been reprinted in a number of collections. See Halsey, Floud and Anderson (1961). In the present book page numbers refer to Parsons (1964).
8. See Savage, S. P. (1980) *The Theories of Talcott Parsons: The Social Relations of Action* for discussion and critique of Parsons' theoretical discourse.
9. 'Cathexis' is a neologism invented by Freud's English translators to translate the German 'Besetzung' (lit. 'investment'). Parsons' use of Freud's concept is discussed further in the present chapter.
10. Published originally in *Psychiatry*, 15:1 (Feb. 1952) and reprinted in Parsons (1964). In the present book page numbers refer to the latter.
11. This paper, written in 1938, is to be found in Parsons (1949).
12. See in particular Parsons (1966 and 1935).
13. See for example, Little and Westergaard (1964). For a more recent account see Scott et al. (1978).
14. See General Register Office (1966) *Classification of Occupations, 1966* (London: HMSO), for example.
15. For a discussion of the consequences for social policy of the 'culture of poverty' thesis see Valentine (1968) especially chapter 3. There is a discussion of IQ testing in chapter 5 of the present book.
16. Little and Westergaard (1964) and Scott et al. (1978).
17. For Bernstein's earlier work as well as more recent work see the three volumes of his *Class, Codes and Control* (1971–3).
18. Rubinstein, D. and Stoneman, C. (Eds), (1970) *Education For Democracy*. In later editions Bernstein's paper appears under the title 'Education Cannot Compensate for Society' but in Bernstein (1970) the earlier title is used.
19. See Cox and Dyson (1969).
20. Newsom, John et al. (1963) *Half Our Future: A Report of the Central Advisory Council for Education (England)* (London: HMSO).
21. Rosen, H. (1972) *Language and Class*, a pamphlet by Falling Wall Press, reprinted in Holly (1974).
22. In contradiction to Bernstein's arguments elsewhere over the previous twenty years.
23. DES and the Scottish Education Department (1978) *Higher Education into the 1990s: A Discussion Document* (London: HMSO).
24. See Neve (1977).
25. See Culley and Demaine (1978) for a discussion of the significance of sociology of education in the training of teachers and the participation of teachers in democratic debate over the curriculum.

## CHAPTER 2

1. The first part of this chapter appeared as part of an article titled 'On the new

sociology of education: A critique of M. F. D. Young and the radical attack on the politics of educational knowledge', *Economy and Society*, 6:2 (May 1977), (Demaine, 1977).

2. This critique of Keddie's arguments was included in a paper titled 'Critique of the Sociology of the Politics of Educational Knowledge' to the British Sociological Association Annual Conference 'Power and the State' at Sheffield University in 1977.

3. See Hirst (1972a) for a discussion of the use of the 'sociology of knowledge' in sociological theory.

4. Pring (1972) for example.

5. Young (1973a and 1973b).

6. Young (1972) p. 213, note 12.

7. For a discussion of Schutz's conception of the essential freedom of the human actor in the social world see Hindess (1972) pp. 17–18. See also Hindess (1977a).

8. The theoretical relation of Schutz to the work of Max Weber is discussed in Hindess (1972 and 1977a).

9. Young (1972) and in Bell and Prescott (1975).

10. The concept of 'structural causality' is elaborated in the paper entitled 'Marx's Immense Theoretical Revolution', in Althusser and Balibar (1970). For a critique see Hindess and Hirst (1975) pp. 272–8 and Cutler et al., Vol. 1 (1977) chapter 7. See also chapter 3 of this present book.

11. There is nothing in Keddie's writings to indicate that teachers do subscribe to the 'myth of cultural deprivation'. This is not a minor problem for a sociology of education concerned with analysis at the level of meanings, expectations, values, attitudes, etc. Keddie's notion that some teachers subscribe to the myth of cultural deprivation does not mean that it can be assumed that others do. She herself warns that such generalizations cannot be made. In her paper 'Classroom Knowledge' in Young (1971), for example, she warns that 'throughout this account references to teachers and pupils are specifically references to teachers and pupils *of this one school*' (p. 134).

12. See Keddie (1973, p. 11) for her account of the 'deficit theory'.

13. 'The Politics of Reading', *Harvard Educational Review*, 40:2 (May 1970) 244–52, and reprinted in Keddie (1973).

14. Labov, William (1969) 'The Logic of Non-Standard English', *Georgetown Monographs on Language and Linguistics* Vol. 22, and Gladwin, Thomas, 'Culture and Logical Process', in Goodenough, Ward (Ed.) (1964) *Explorations in Cultural Anthropology*, both reprinted in Keddie (1973). Cf. Valentine (1968) especially chapters 1 and 3.

15. Melanesian islanders, see Gladwin above.

16. See Kingdom (1976) for a discussion of political education.

17. Keddie warns against romanticism herself.

18. See Leach (1969, 1974, 1977 and 1978).

## CHAPTER 3

1. See the paper 'Ideology and Ideological State Apparatuses' in Althusser (1971) reprinted in Cosin (1972). In the present book, page numbers for this article refer to Althusser (1971). See Hirst (1976a and 1976b) for critique of Althusser's

theory of ideology and Hirst (1972b) for critique of Jacques Ranicière's and Louis Althusser's theories of ideology.

2. See Şavage (1979) for a non-epistemological critique of the theories of Talcott Parsons. Parsons' work in educational theory is discussed in chapter 1 of the present book.

3. Cf. Dahrendorf, Ralf (1959) *Class and Class Conflict in Industrial Society*. For Dahrendorf and others the class struggle of which Marx writes has been superseded by class conflict in post-capitalist societies. For a sociological critique of the 'post-capitalist' thesis see Westergaard, John H., 'Sociology: the Myth of Classlessness' in Blackburn, R. (Ed.) (1972) *Ideology in Social Science*.

4. See for example Engels, F. (1968), *The Origin of the Family, Private Property and the State*, 'the modern representative state is an instrument of exploitation of wage labour by capital' (pp. 587−8).

5. This is something of a misnomer for the maintained sector of the British education system. Of course, the notion of a 'maintained' sector appears in the context of a situation in which there is an 'independent' sector. The actual status of the latter is such that the term 'independent' is itself something of a misnomer. For instance, many of the teachers in the 'independent' sector were educated within the maintained sector and most attended state maintained universities and/or colleges of education. Furthermore, the charitable status of much of the independent sector means that it is in effect subsidized by the Treasury by the absence of taxation on profits from investment funds.

6. The ISAs are *unified* in another sense, that is, by their function. 'The unity of the ideological apparatuses lies outside them, in the ideological unity of the ruling class' (see Hirst, 1976b, p. 394).

7. See Berkeley, *Treatise Concerning the Principles of Human Knowledge* (1710) for example.

8. See Hume's *Enquiry Concerning the Human Understanding* (1748). Of course, the classical Marxist critique of Hume, Berkeley and 'idealism' is Lenin's *Materialism and Empirio-Criticism* (1909).

9. See Althusser's paper 'From "Capital" to Marx's Philosophy', section 10 in particular, in Part I of Althusser and Balibar (1970).

10. Lacan, J. (1968) 'The Mirror Phase', *New Left Review*, No. 51.

11. See Hirst (1976b). Also see Hindess and Hirst (1977) and Cutler et al., *Marx's 'Capital' and Capitalism Today*, Vol. 1 and 2 (1977 and 1978 respectively), for discussion of non-subjective forms of economic agency.

12. Althusser and Balibar (1970).

13. For a critique of the Marxist concept of 'mode of production' see Hindess and Hirst (1977). For a critique of the notion of 'structural causality' see Hindess and Hirst (1975) pp. 272−8. The concept of structural causality is elaborated in the paper titled 'Marx's Immense Theoretical Revolution', in Althusser and Balibar (1970).

14. Cf. Hindess, 'Humanism and Teleology in Sociological Theory', in Hindess, B. (Ed.) (1977) *Sociological Theories of the Economy*.

15. See Young (1973b), p. 216. For both Young and Freire cultural action is political action, see Young (1972, 1973b and 1975a). For a critique see Demaine (1977).

16. It is rare to find any serious analysis of his *theory* in these references.

17. Young is content to ignore this debate.

18. Cf. Baran, P. A. (1973) *The Political Economy of Growth* and Baran, P. A. and. Sweezy, P. M. (1970) *Monopoly Capital*.
19. Cf. Frank, A. G. (1971) *Capitalism and Underdevelopment in Latin America*.
20. For this see Culley, L. A. (1977) 'Economic Development in Neo-Marxist Theory' in Hindess, B. (Ed.) *Sociological Theories of the Economy*, and Laclau, E. (1971) 'Feudalism and Capitalism in Latin America', *New Left Review*, No. 67.
21. For a clear example of the anti-dialogical process we need look no further than the work of Freire himself. Consider his references to Hegel's *The Phenomenology of Mind*. Freire tells us that 'what characterises the oppressed is their subordination to the consciousness of the master, as Hegel affirms . . .' (Freire, 1972a). Hegel, of course, affirms nothing of the sort, for he is not concerned with the 'characteristics of the oppressed' as Freire would have his student believe, but rather with the forms or modes of consciousness. The Bondsman in Hegel's discourse is not the oppressed in Freire's discourse and likewise the Master to which Hegel refers is not the oppressor to which Freire refers. In *The Phenomenology of Mind* the Bondsman is a form of 'self-consciousness in the broad sense' whilst the Master is also a form or mode of consciousness, in this case 'the consciousness that exists *for itself*'. Friere engages in no discussion here. Moreover, he is quite inaccurate.
22. See especially Freire (1974) but the concept appears throughout his work.
23. Weber, M. (1968) *Economy and Society*, Vol. 3, p. 1116.
24. The concept of 'alienation' is commonly used in certain branches of contemporary sociology of education. See, for example, the work of Bowles and Gintis and the critique of the use of the concept of alienation in chapter 5 of the present book.

## CHAPTER 4

1. See Gintis' paper, 'Towards a Political Economy of Education: A Radical Critique of Ivan Illich's *Deschooling Society*', *Harvard Educational Review*, 42:1 (Feb. 1972).
2. Young claims that he is a radical and that he is committed to 'an idea of human liberation' (Young, 1973b, p. 210). Explicitly he rejects 'turning to the easy slogans of "deschooling", "free schools", or the currently fashionable "community school"' (1973a, p. 11). Here, he appears to contradict his position in his paper 'On the Politics of Educational Knowledge' but as we have seen in chapter 2 his rejection of formal education as the imposition of meanings and his general arguments concerning the character of knowledge and the subjective meanings of pupils, is consistent with favourable reference to Illich's *Deschooling Society*, and with the insistence on the primacy of pupils' subjective meaning which is common to all three forms of schooling mentioned above. With regard to the primacy of the subjective meanings of pupils I would agree with Bernstein's conclusions that although 'the social experience the child already possesses is valid and significant, and that this social experience should be reflected back to him as being valid and significant' (Bernstein, 1970, p. 120), this experience can only be the *starting point* to a wider education. The point is that education should not be *restricted* to such experience and meanings. For Young, of course, anything other than this restriction involves the 'imposition of meanings'.

3. Illich argues that 'Today all schools are obligatory, open-ended, and competitive. The same convergence in institutional style affects health care,
merchandising, personnel administration, and political life. All these institutional processes tend to pile up at the manipulative end of the spectrum.'
Other institutions have 'become bureaucratic, self-justifying, and manipulative.
The same thing happened to systems of social security, to labor unions, major
churches and diplomacies, the care of the aged, and the disposal of the dead.'
(Illich, 1971, p. 61).

4. These are to be found on the left of the spectrum and they are to be 'distinguished
by spontaneous use' because 'Telephone link-ups, subway lines, mail routes,
public markets and exchanges do not require hard or soft sells to induce their
clients to use them. Sewage systems, drinking water, parks, and sidewalks *are
institutions* men use without having to be institutionally convinced that it is to
their advantage to do so.' (Illich, 1971, pp. 54–5.) For a further discussion see
Illich's *Tools of Conviviality*.

5. The operational problems of education in a deschooled society are discussed in
Illich, 1971, *passim*. For an example and an amusing description of the solution to
one problem see Illich's description of the 'coffee shop' meeting (ibid., p. 21). For
a more recent discussion of deschooling see Illich (1974).

## CHAPTER 5

1. *Harvard Educational Review*, 42:1 (Feb. 1972).
2. In this respect Bowles and Gintis' work proposes notions similar to those in the
work of Braverman (1974).
3. See Tony Cutler's review of Braverman in his paper 'The romance of "labour" ',
*Economy and Society*, 7:1 (Feb. 1978).
4. See chapter 3 for a critique of this notion, and in particular see Cutler, et al. (1977
and 1978).
5. See note 1.
6. This article is to be found in *Economy and Society*, 5: 4 (Nov. 1976). Sections of
the article are reprinted in Gleeson (1977). Page numbers refer to the former.
7. See, for example, Robinson (1976).
8. Educational policy is part of social policy and as such it is subject to political
control and political 'determination'.
9. *Harvard Educational Review*, 39:1 (1969).
10. See Owen, L. and Stoneman, C., 'Education and the Nature of Intelligence', in
Rubinstein, D. and Stoneman, C. (Eds) (1970) *Education for Democracy*,
p. 78.
11. See Hudson, L., 'The Context of the Debate', in Richardson, K. and Spears, D.
(Eds) (1972) *Race, Culture and Intelligence*, p. 12.
12. Jensen himself considers that 'Compensatory education has been tried and it
apparently has failed (despite) unprecedented support from Federal funds' and he
has also stated that he wants 'increased emphasis on these efforts, in the spirit of
experimentation'. See Owen and Stoneman, op. cit., p. 78.
13. Norwood, Sir Cyril et al. (1943) *Curriculum and Examinations in Secondary
Schools: A report of the Committee of the Secondary Schools Examination Council*,
London: HMSO. It was the influence of the Norwood Report which led to the

selection of children at 11 + as the basis of the tripartite system in secondary education. See Bernbaum (1967), chapter 6.

14. Bernbaum (1967), p. 113.
15. In Richardson and Spears (1972), pp. 36—55.
16. Bowles, Gintis and Meyer, 'Education, IQ, and the legitimation of the social division of labor', *Berkeley Journal of Sociology*, xx (1975—6) 233—64.
17. Popper makes the point that 'A host of interesting problems is raised by *operationalism*, the doctrine that theoretical concepts have to be defined in terms of measuring operations. Against this view, it can be shown that measurements *presuppose theories*. There is no measurement without a theory and no operation which can be satisfactorily described in non-theoretical terms. The attempts to do so are always circular' (*Conjectures and Refutations: The Growth of Scientific Knowledge*, p. 62). For a critique of Popper's Theory of Science see chapter 6 in Hindess (1977a).
18. Because IQ is an ordinal scale the scores cannot be used arithmetically. There is no justification for the common practice of calculating 'average IQ' scores from individual scores.
19. Psychometric testing is still used in the form of 'scholastic aptitude' tests in some comprehensive schools.

## CHAPTER 6

1. Published in the Penguin 90th birthday edition of *The Black Girl in Search of God* (1946). Quoted in the paper by Michael Barratt Brown, Ken Coates and Tony Topham titled 'Workers' Control Versus "Revolutionary" Theory' in Miliband, R. and Saville, J. (Eds), *The Socialist Register 1975*, pp. 298—9.
2. This remains the case. See Philip Robinson's excellent book *Education and Poverty* (1976).
3. The Open University, which draws a large number of its students from the ranks of the teaching profession, at one time recommended *Knowledge and Control* as a Set Book. Young's work has, therefore, been available to practising teachers as well as teachers in training.
4. See Young and Whitty (1977), p. 1, and for a wider discussion of the distinction between education and schooling see Richmond (1975).
5. Frith, S. and Corrigan, P., 'The Politics of Education' in Young and Whitty (1977), pp. 253—68.
6. 'Leave curriculum planning to the professionals' in *The Teacher* (Newspaper of the National Union of Teachers), 31 March 1978, p. 5. The article is a report of the NUT Annual Conference and in particular the debate over 'curriculum control' at the conference.
7. Delegate to the NUT conference reported in *The Teacher*, ibid.
8. *A New Partnership for Our Schools*: Report of the Committee of Enquiry appointed jointly by the Secretary of State for Education and Science and the Secretary of State for Wales under the chairmanship of Mr Tom Taylor, CBE. (London: HMSO, 1977).
9. *The William Tyndale Junior and Infants Schools*: Report of the Public Inquiry conducted by Mr Robin Auld, QC into the teaching, organization and

management of the William Tyndale Junior and Infants Schools Islington, London, N1. (London: ILEA, 1976).

10. See White, John P. (1977) 'Tyndale and the Left', *Forum for the Discussion of New Trends in Education*, 19:2.

11. See Whitty and Young (Eds) (1976) *Explorations in the Politics of School Knowledge*, p. 5, for example.

12. For a discussion of industrial democracy see *Report of the Royal Commission on Industrial Democracy*, Chairman, Lord Bullock, Cmnd., 6706 (London: HMSO, 1977).

13. For further discussion see for example the Conclusion to Cutler et al., Vol. 2 (1978).

14. See, for example, Hodgson (1975) for discussion and critique.

15. As we have already pointed out in the introduction, Marx's own formulations in the 1859 Preface to *A Contribution to the Critique of Political Economy* lead those who take them seriously to political abstentionism.

16. See Hussain (1976).

17. We have already said that part of such a policy is the struggle for equality of educational opportunity.

18. Little and Westergaard (1964), Scott et al. (1978), for example.

19. See Kingdom, E. F. (1976) 'Political Education', *Research in Education* (November).

20. *The Teacher*, 31 March 1978. See note 6.

21. Cf. Kogan (1978).

22. In the struggle to reorganize secondary education for example.

23. Taylor (1977).

24. Op. cit., see note 6.

25. Ibid.

26. In particular there are a whole range of issues concerning the concept of representation which go beyond the issues raised below. There are clearly problems of assessing different possible *mechanisms* of democratic control. Clearly, different mechanisms can have significantly different consequences for policy and for policy implementation. As I suggest below, the Taylor committee recommendations should be seen as a first step *towards* democracy in education rather than an end in themselves.

27. See Hussain (1976) for example.

28. For an interesting discussion see Poulantzas, N. (1978) 'Towards a Democratic Socialism', *New Left Review*, No. 109 (May/June).

29. Ibid.

30. With respect to education Neve (1977) is informative.

31. *The Teacher*, op. cit. (note 6, above). See also the NUT pamphlet, *Management and Government of Schools: National Union of Teachers' Evidence to the Taylor Committee of Inquiry* (1975).

# Bibliography

Althusser, L. (1969) *For Marx*. London: Allen Lane, The Penguin Press.
—— (1971) *Lenin and Philosophy, and Other Essays*. London: New Left Books.
Althusser, L. and Balibar, E. (1970) *Reading Capital*. London: New Left Books.
Auld, R. (1976) *The William Tyndale Junior and Infants Schools*. London: Inner London Education Authority.
Banks, O. (1971) *The Sociology of Education*, 2nd ed. London: Batsford.
Baran, P. A. (1973) *The Political Economy of Growth*. Harmondsworth: Penguin Books.
Baran, P. A. and Sweezy, P. M. (1970) *Monopoly Capital*. Harmondsworth: Penguin Books.
Bell, R. and Prescott, W. (Eds) (1975) *The Schools Council: A Second Look*. London: Ward Lock.
Berger, P. L. and Berger, B. (1976) *Sociology: A Biographical Approach*. Harmondsworth: Penguin Books.
Bernbaum, G. (1967) *Social Change and the Schools, 1918–1944*. London: Routledge and Kegan Paul.
Bernstein, B. (1970) 'A Critique of the Concept of "Compensatory Education"', in Rubinstein and Stoneman (1970).
—— (1971–3) *Class, Codes and Control*, 3 Vols. London and Boston: Routledge and Kegan Paul.
Blackburn, R. (Ed.) (1972) *Ideology in Social Science*. London: Collins.
Bowles, S. and Gintis, H. (1976) *Schooling in Capitalist America*. London: Routledge and Kegan Paul.
Bowles, S., Gintis, H. and Meyer, P. (1975–6) 'Education, IQ, and the Legitimation of the Social Division of Labor', *Berkeley Journal of Sociology*, XX.
Braverman, H. (1974) *Labor and Monopoly Capital*. London and New York: Monthly Review Press.
Brown, M. and Baldwin, S. (Eds) (1977) *The Year Book of Social Policy 1977*. London: Routledge and Kegan Paul.

Bullock, Lord, et al., (1977) *Report of the Royal Commission on Industrial Democracy*, Cmnd. 6706. London: HMSO.

Centre For Contemporary Cultural Studies (1977) *Working Papers in Cultural Studies 10: On Ideology*. University of Birmingham.

Cosin, B. R. (Ed.) (1972) *Education: Structure and Society*. Harmondsworth: Penguin Books.

Cox, C. B. and Dyson, A. E. (1969a) *Fight for Education* (A Black Paper). London: The Critical Quarterly Society.

—— (1969b) *The Crisis in Education* (A Black Paper). London: The Critical Quarterly Society.

Culley, L. A. (1977) 'Economic Development in Neo-Marxist Theory', in Hindess (1977b).

—— Culley, L. A. and Demaine, J. (1978) 'Sociology of Education and the Education of Teachers: a critique of D. R. McNamara', *Educational Studies*, 4:3.

Cutler, A. J. (1978) 'The romance of "labour"', *Economy and Society*, 7:1.

Cutler, A. J., Hindess, B., Hirst, P. Q. and Hussain, A. (1977 and 1978) *Marx's 'Capital' and Capitalism Today*, Vols 1 and 2, London: Routledge and Kegan Paul.

David, M. (1977) 'Parents and educational politics in 1977' in Brown, M. and Baldwin, S. (Eds.) (1977).

Dahrendorf, R. (1959) *Class and Class Conflict in Industrial Society*. London: Routledge and Kegan Paul.

Demaine, J. (1977) 'On the new sociology of education: A critique of M. F. D. Young and the radical attack on the politics of educational knowledge', *Economy and Society*, 6:2.

—— (1979) 'Sociological theories of ideology and education'. PhD thesis: The University of Liverpool.

Department of Education and Science and the Scottish Education. Department (1978) *Higher Education into the 1990s: A Discussion Document*. London: HMSO.

Diamond, Lord, et al. (1975) *Royal Commission on the Distribution of Income and Wealth*, Report No. 1, Cmnd. 6171. London: HMSO.

Douglas, J. W. B. (1964) *The Home and The School*. London: MacGibbon and Kee.

Durkheim, E. (1964) *The Rules of Sociological Method*, 8th ed. New York: The Free Press.

—— (1956) *Education and Sociology*. Glencoe, Illinois: The Free Press.

Engels, F. (1968) *The Origin of the Family, Private Property and the State* in Marx, K. and Engels, F., *Selected Works in One Volume*. London: Lawrence and Wishart.

Eysenck, H. J. (1971) *Race, Intelligence and Education*. London: Temple Smith.

Filmer, P. et al. (1972) *New Directions in Sociological Theory*. New York: Collier-Macmillan.

Finn, D., Grant, N. and Johnson, R. (1977) 'Social Democracy, Education and the Crisis' in Centre For Contemporary Cultural Studies (1977).

Flude, M. and Ahier, J. (Eds) (1974) *Educability, Schools and Ideology*. London: Croom Helm.

Frank, A. G. (1971) *Capitalism and Underdevelopment in Latin America*. Harmondsworth: Penguin Books.

Freire, P. (1970a) 'The Adult Literacy Process as Cultural Action for Freedom', *Harvard Educational Review*, 40:2.

—— (1970b) 'Cultural Action and Conscientization', *Harvard Educational Review*, 40:3.

—— (1972a) *Pedagogy of the Oppressed*. Harmondsworth: Penguin Books.

—— (1972b) *Cultural Action for Freedom* (a reprint of 1970a and 1970b with an introduction by the author). Harmondsworth: Penguin Books.

—— (1974) *Education for Critical Consciousness*. London: Sheed and Ward.

Galton, F. (1869) *Hereditary Genius*. London: Macmillan.

Gintis, H. (1972) 'Towards a Political Economy of Education: A Radical Critique of Ivan Illich's *Deschooling Society*', *Harvard Educational Review*, 42:1.

Gladwin, T. (1964) 'Culture and logical process', in Goodenough (1964).

Gleeson, D. (Ed.) (1977) *Identity and Structure: Issues in the Sociology of Education*. Driffield: Nafferton Books.

Goodenough, W. (Ed.) (1964) *Explorations in Cultural Anthropology*. New York: McGraw-Hill.

Gorbutt, D. (1972) 'The New Sociology of Education', *Education for Teaching* (Autumn 1972).

Halsey, A. H., Floud, J. and Anderson, C. A. (Eds) (1961) *Education, Economy and Society*. New York: The Free Press.

Hegel, G. W. F. (1910) *The Phenomenology of Mind*. Trans. by J. B. Baillie. London and New York: The Macmillan Company.

Hindess, B. (1972) 'The "phenomenological" sociology of Alfred Schutz', *Economy and Society*, 1:1.

—— (1977a) *Philosophy and Methodology in the Social Sciences*. Brighton: Harvester Press.

—— (Ed.) (1977b) *Sociological Theories of the Economy*. London: Macmillan.

Hindess, B. and Hirst, P. Q. (1975) *Pre-Capitalist Modes of Production*. London: Routledge and Kegan Paul.

—— (1977) *Mode of Production and Social Formation*. London: Macmillan.

Hirst, P. Q. (1972a) 'Recent tendencies in sociological theory', *Economy and Society*, 1:2.

—— (1972b) 'A Critique of Jacques Rancière's and Louis Althusser's Theories of Ideology' (unpublished mimeo).

—— (1975) *Durkheim, Bernard and Epistemology*. London: Routledge and Kegan Paul.

—— (1976a) *Problems and Advances in the Theory of Ideology*. Cambridge: Cambridge University Communist Party.

—— (1976b) 'Althusser and the Theory of Ideology', *Economy and Society*, 5:4.

Hodgson, Geoff (1975) *Trotsky and Fatalistic Marxism*. Nottingham: Spokesman Books.

Holly, D. (Ed.) (1974) *Education or Domination?* London: Arrow Books.

Hudson, L. (1972) 'The context of the debate' in Richardson & Spears (Eds.).

Hussain, A. (1976) 'The economy and the educational system in capitalist societies', *Economy and Society*, 5:4.

Illich, I. D. (1971) *Deschooling Society*. London: Calder and Boyars.

—— (1974) *After Deschooling What?* London: The Writers' and Readers' Publishing Cooperative.

—— (1973) *Tools of Conviviality*. London: Calder and Boyars.

Jackson, B. and Marsden, D. (1962) *Education and the Working Class*. London: Routledge and Kegan Paul.

Kamin, L. J. (1975) *The Science and Politics of IQ*. New York: John Wiley.

Keddie, N. (Ed.) (1973) *Tinker, Tailor . . . The Myth of Cultural Deprivation*. Harmondsworth: Penguin Books.

Kingdom, E. F. (1976) 'Political Education', *Research in Education* (November).

Kogan, M. (1978) *The Politics of Educational Change*. London: Fontana Books.

Labov, W. (1969) 'The Logic of Non-Standard English', *Georgetown Monographs on Language and Linguistics*, Vol. 22. Reprinted in Goodenough (1964).

Lacan, J. (1968) 'The Mirror Phase', *New Left Review*, No. 51.

Laclau, E. (1971) 'Feudalism and Capitalism in Latin America', *New Left Review*, No. 67.

Leach, E. (1969) 'Education for What?', Roscoe Lecture, Manchester University, April 1969.

—— (1974) 'Freedom and Social Conditioning', Raymond Priestley Lecture, University of Birmingham, October, 1974.

—— (1977) 'Literacy be damned', *Observer*, 20 February.

—— (1978) 'The Disutility of Literacy', Loughborough University, April 1978.

Lenin, V. I. (1902) *What is to be Done?*, reprinted in *Collected Works*, Vol. 5. Moscow: FLPH.

—— (1909) *Materialism and Empirio-Criticism*, reprinted in *Collected Works*, Vol. 14. Moscow: FLPH.

—— (1919) *The State*, reprinted in *Collected Works*, Vol. 29. Moscow: FLPH.

—— (1921) *The New Economic Policy and the Tasks of the Political Education Departments: Report to the Second All-Russia Congress of Political Education Departments*, 17 October 1921, reprinted in *Collected Works*, Vol. 33.

—— (1975) *On Public Education*. Moscow: Progress Publishers.

Levitas, M. (1974) *Marxist Perspectives in the Sociology of Education*. London: Routledge and Kegan Paul.

Little, A. and Westergaard, J. H. (1964) 'The Trend of Class Differentials in Educational Opportunity in England and Wales', *British Journal of Sociology*, XV.

Lukacs, G. (1971) *History and Class Consciousness*. London: Merlin Press.

Manzer, R. A. (1970) *Teachers and Politics*. Manchester University Press.

Marx, K. (1859) Preface to *A Contribution to the Critique of Political Economy*, in Marx, K. and Engels, F., *Selected Works in One Volume*. London: Lawrence and Wishart, 1968.

—— (1871) *The Civil War in France*, in *Selected Works* (op. cit.).

—— (1875) *Critique of the Gotha Programme*, in *Selected Works* (op. cit.).

—— (1867, 1885, 1894) *Capital*, Vols 1–3. Moscow: FLPH, 1954–9.

Marx, K. and Engels, F. (1846) *The German Ideology*. English trans. London: Lawrence and Wishart, 1965.

—— (1848) *The Communist Manifesto*, in *Selected Works* (op. cit.).

Mead, G. H. (1934) *Mind, Self and Society*. University of Chicago Press.

Miliband, R. and Saville, J. (Eds) *The Socialist Register 1975*. London: Merlin Press.

National Union of Teachers (1975) *Management and Government of Schools: National Union of Teachers' Evidence to the Taylor Committee of Inquiry*. A pamphlet with Foreword by Fred Jarvis, General Secretary.

Neve, B. (1977) 'Bureaucracy and Politics in Local Government: The Role of Local Authority Education Officers' *Public Administration* (Autumn).

Newsom, John H. et al. (1963) *Half Our Future, a report of the Central Advisory Council for Education (England)*. London: HMSO.

Newson, J. and E. (1976) *Seven Years Old in the Home Environment*. London: George Allen and Unwin.

Norwood, Cyril et al. (1943) *Curriculum and Examinations in Secondary Schools: A report of the Committee of the Secondary Schools Examination Council.* London: HMSO.

Parsons, T. (1935) 'The Place of Ultimate Values in Sociological Theory', *International Journal of Ethics*, No. 45.

—— (1938) 'The Role of Ideas in Social Action', *American Sociological Review*, No. 3. Reprinted in Parsons (1949).

—— (1949) *Essays in Sociological Theory.* Glencoe, Illinois: The Free Press.

—— (1951) *The Social System.* Glencoe, Illinois: The Free Press.

—— (1952) 'The Superego and the Theory of Social Systems', originally published in *Psychiatry*, 15:1 (February 1952) and reprinted in Parsons (1964).

—— (1959) 'The School Class as a Social System: Some of its Functions in American Society', *Harvard Educational Review*, 29:4, reprinted in Parsons (1964).

—— (1964) *The Social Structure and Personality.* New York: The Free Press.

—— (1966) *Societies: Evolutionary and Comparative Perspectives.* Englewood Cliffs, New Jersey: Prentice-Hall.

Parsons, T. and Shils, E. A., (1962) *Towards a General Theory of Action.* New York: Harper and Row.

Popper, K. R. (1963) *Conjectures and Refutations: The Growth of Scientific Knowledge.* London: Routledge and Kegan Paul.

Postman, N. (1970) 'The politics of reading', *Harvard Educational Review*, 40:2, reprinted in Keddie (1973).

Poulantzas, N. (1978) 'Towards a Democratic Socialism', *New Left Review*, No. 109.

Pring, R. (1972) 'Knowledge out of Control', *Education for Teaching*, No. 89.

Reimer, E. (1971) *School is Dead: An Essay on Alternatives in Education.* Harmondsworth: Penguin Books.

Richardson, K. and Spears, D. (Eds) (1972) *Race, Culture and Intelligence.* Harmondsworth: Penguin Books.

Richmond, W. K. (1975) *Education and Schooling.* London: Methuen.

Robinson, P. (1976) *Education and Poverty.* London: Methuen.

Rosen, H. (1972) *Language and Class.* A Falling Wall Press pamphlet. Reprinted in Holly, D. (Ed.) (1974) *Education or Domination?* London: Arrow Books.

Rubinstein, D. and Stoneman, C. (Eds) (1970) *Education For Democracy.* Harmondsworth: Penguin Books.

Ryan, J. (1972) 'IQ – The Illusion of Objectivity', in Richardson and Spears (1972).

Savage, S. P. (1980) *The Theories of Talcott Parsons: The Social Relations of Action*. London: Macmillan.

Schutz, A. (1962) *Collected Papers I: The Problem of Social Reality*. The Hauge: Nijhoff.

—— (1964) *Collected Papers II: Studies in Social Theory*. The Hauge: Nijhoff.

—— (1966) *Collected Papers III: Studies in Phenomenological Philosophy*. The Hague: Nijhoff.

—— (1967) *The Phenomenology of the Social World*. Evanston: Northwestern: University Press.

Scott, P. et al. (1978) 'The working class in higher and further education', *The Times Higher Education Supplement*, 20 Jan.

Secretary of State for Education and Science and the Secretary of State for Wales, (1977) *Education in Schools: A Consultative Document*. (A Green Paper) Cmnd. 6869. London: HMSO.

Taylor, Tom, et al. (1977) *A New Partnership For Our Schools* (Department of Education and Science and Welsh Office). London: HMSO.

*The Teacher* (1978) 'Leave Curriculum Planning to the Professionals, Conference Urges', 31 March.

Tort, M. (1977) *Le Quotient Intellectuel*, Paris, Maspero.

Valentine, C. A. (1968) *Culture and Poverty: Critique and Counter-Proposals*. University of Chicago Press.

Weber, M. (1968) *Economy and Society*. New York: Bedminster Press.

Westergaard, J. H. (1964) 'Sociology: the Myth of Classlessness', in Blackburn (1972).

White, J. P. (1977) 'Tyndale and the Left', *Forum for the Discussion of New Trends in Education*, 19:2.

Whitty, G. and Young, M. F. D. (Eds) (1976) *Explorations in the Politics of School Knowledge*. Nafferton: studies in Education Ltd.

Willer, D. and J. (1973) *Systematic Empiricism: critique of a pseudoscience*. Englewood Cliffs, New Jersey: Prentice-Hall.

Young, M. F. D. (Ed.) (1971) *Knowledge and Control: New Directions for the Sociology of Education*. London: Collier-Macmillan.

—— (1972) 'On the Politics of Educational Knowledge', *Economy and Society*, 1:2.

—— (1973a) 'Educational Theorizing: A Radical Alternative', *Education for Teaching* (Summer).

—— (1973b) 'Taking Sides Against the Probable: Problems of Relativism and Commitment in Teaching and the Sociology of Knowledge', *Educational Review*, 25:3.

—— (1975a) 'Curriculum Change: Limits and Possibilities', *Educational Studies*, 1:2.

—— (1975b) 'Sociologists and the politics of comprehensive education',
*Forum for the Discussion of New Trends in Education* (Summer).
Young, M. F. D. and Whitty, G. (Eds) (1977) *Society, State and Schooling.*
Brighton: The Falmer Press.

# Index

X